The Dog Decoder

How to Identify Any Dog, Any Time

The Dog Decoder

How to Identify Any Dog, Any Time

David Alderton
foreword by Bruce Fogle

THUNDER BAY
P·R·E·S·S

San Diego, California

Thunder Bay Press
An imprint of Printers Row Publishing Group
10350 Barnes Canyon Road, Suite 100, San Diego, CA 92121
www.thunderbaybooks.com

Printers Row Publishing Group is a division of Readerlink Distribution Services, LLC.
Thunder Bay Press is a registered trademark of Readerlink Distribution Services, LLC.

All notations of errors or omissions should be addressed to Thunder Bay Press, Editorial Department, at the above address. All other correspondence (author inquiries, permissions) concerning the content of this book should be addressed to Moseley Road Inc., info@moseleyroad.com

Thunder Bay Press
Publisher: Peter Norton
Associate Publisher: Ana Parker
Publishing/Editorial Team: April Farr, Vicki Jaeger, Tanja Fijalkowski, Kathryn C. Dalby, Carrie Davis
Editorial Team: JoAnn Padgett, Melinda Allman, Dan Mansfield
Production Team: Jonathan Lopes, Rusty von Dyl

Produced by Moseley Road Inc., www.moseleyroad.com
President: Sean Moore
Production Director: Adam Moore

Library of Congress Cataloging-in-Publication data is available upon request.
ISBN: 978-1-68412-559-3

Printed in China
22 21 20 19 18   1 2 3 4 5

Contents

Why We Love Them by Bruce Fogle

This much I know: During the time I've been a clinical veterinarian, and that's almost 40 years, no dog has been more upwardly mobile than the ubiquitous mutt. Once he was the poor man's dog, the "cottager's dog," as he was called in Victorian England. Mutts were the result then, as they mostly still are now, of unauthorized alliances, the progeny of freethinking dogs who simply did as nature intended, rather than as we imposed.

The elevation of the mutt from mongrel, Heinz 57, mixed breed, to star status, is a curious consequence of our evolving relationship with the natural world around us. In my early years as a vet, purebred dogs were simply too expensive for many people to buy. And when a breeder's purebred dog accidentally mated with a dog of another breed, the resulting crossbred pups were either

drowned at birth or given to dog shelters or dog pounds. Mutts were free of charge and instantly available—no questions asked. They were the pets of poor families or those who thought they might want a dog but didn't want one enough to spend money on it.

As spendable income became more available, some working class families moved on to purebred dogs. But something else, quite curious, also happened. The mutt started to become fashionable. I'll give you an analogy from veterinary medicine to explain why.

Up until the 1960s, when I was a veterinary student, veterinary medicine was a man's profession—a rural man's profession. In the 1970s, veterinary schools started accepting students according to merit, not sex. At the same time, students from an urban background started to apply and attend.

This had a profound effect on the ethos of veterinary medicine. When I studied—I shudder to think how mindless we all were then—we carried out weekly "surgical exercises" on mutts provided by the local pound. In the 1970s, the influx of new students balked at doing so. They just said, "No!" They brought a different culture to veterinary education, an urban and more empathetic culture, in which care and compassion were more important than weight-per-day-of-age and market prices. In this culture, a mutt had as much value as a dog show prize winner.

These new students brought with them thoughts and ideas that were starting to percolate through what, at the time, was only a small section of society. How are we treating the natural world around us? What are we doing to the natural world around us? How can it be true that only humans have feelings and emotions while animals have just instincts? Are humans truly unique and separate from the rest of the animal world, or are we part of it?

Our rapidly changing attitude about the world around us affected our attitude toward our pets, and this was beneficial to mutts in three ways. First, dogs were seen as a respected species, as worthy of serious study as any other animal species. Second, mutts were considered by some as 'more natural' than purebreds, the result of natural selection rather than arbitrary human intervention. Some people involved in animal welfare were downright embarrassed to be seen in public with a purebred dog. (That was truly "sleeping with the enemy.") And third, mutts were seen as medically healthier than many purebreds, for it was rapidly emerging that, while creating breeds for specific looks and abilities, we had also unwittingly increased the incidence of specific inherited disorders in almost every breed—certainly in the breeds that were developed from a small gene pool.

I'm involved with Hearing Dogs for Deaf People, a charity that rescues young unwanted dogs from shelters and retrains them to act as ears for hearing-impaired people. Twenty-five years ago, we had no difficulty finding prospective Hearing Dogs. Shelters were bulging with little mutts. No longer. Today, we travel abroad to find our stars. We need to do so because people have become more responsible about caring for their dogs, so fewer of them end up in shelters, and because we have to compete with so many prospective dog owners who want to rescue a dog and give a mutt a good home. The reactive, alert, intelligent dogs we need are often gone the day they arrive.

The desire of so many families to have a mutt rather than a purebred is now so great that a new breeding industry has emerged: the intentional mutt, the crossbred breed, the "designer dog," such as the Puggle, the Cockapoo, and the Labradoodle. I'm in favor. I'm in favor because crossbreeding dilutes potentially deleterious genes that adversely affect health, while still making it easy to guess the physical type and personality of the adult dog.

The advantage of knowing your mutt's background is that certain aspects of his behavior are likely to be increased or diminished, based on the breeds that contributed to his mix. And that's where this book comes in. Because if you have a dog who's part terrier, you won't be surprised when he starts digging up the garden. A mutt with some sighthound in him is more likely to chase the cat. And a shepherd mix will want to herd your kids.

The mutt's future? Who knows. Mutts are created by opportunist canines, but also by irresponsible dog owners. Forty years ago, the mutts I saw had terrier, hound, or sheepdog ancestry. Today they are more likely to have Bull Terrier or Rottweiler ancestry. Creating mutts by crossing breeds? I'm in favor. After all, that's how most of the breeds of today were once developed. But irresponsible dog owners? When I'm in charge, I'll have them attend compulsory dog parenting classes and take exams before they can share their home with a dog.

Why Spay or Neuter Your Dog?

Thousands and thousands of dogs lose their lives each year because there aren't enough homes who want them and enough space in shelters to keep them. And it will always be so, as long as we keep breeding dogs casually.

Breeding dogs is a serious undertaking that should only be part of a well-planned program. Why? Because dogs pass on their physical and behavioral problems to their offspring. Even healthy, well-behaved dogs can pass on genetic problems. It's a common misconception that mutts are free from the genetic defects that plague their purebred cousins. Yes, the larger the gene pool, the less chance that two mutant genes will randomly collide. But the fact is that mutts get all the diseases purebred dogs get. And just because a dog is healthy doesn't mean she doesn't have a defective gene lurking in her DNA.

Is your dog so sweet that you'd like to have a litter of puppies just like her? If only it were that easy! But if you breed her to another dog, the pups will not have the same genetic heritage she has. Let's face it: Most mutts are not the offspring of a clandestine liaison between two purebred dogs; rather, they're a mix of many, many crosses. How are you going to figure out the precise mix that produced her, and then find a male who offers that exact same mix? It's impossible.

Breeding her *parents* again will increase the odds of a similar pup, but even then, the puppies in the second litter could inherit different genes. In fact, the only way to make a dog who is just like another dog, genetically speaking, is by cloning. And even then, the canine clone would be physically identical but behaviorally very different, because canine personalities, just like those of humans, are the result of complex interactions between genetics and environment.

What does this all mean? *There is no way to breed a dog who is just like another dog.* Each dog is a unique individual.

Plus, when you spay your female:
- You avoid her heat cycles, during which she discharges blood and scent.
- You greatly reduce her risk of developing mammary cancer, and eliminate the risk of pyometra and uterine cancer.
- You prevent unwanted pregnancies.

When you neuter your male:
- You curb his desire to roam and to fight with other males.
- You greatly reduce his risk of developing prostate cancer and eliminate the risk of testicular cancer.
- You reduce his leg lifting and mounting behavior.

World Map of Breeds

When and where dogs were first domesticated is still hotly debated, but there is no doubt that some breeds are very ancient. Variation in these dogs was probably due mostly to the variation in the wolves they descended from. But as domestic dogs traveled with their human companions, they adapted or were bred to suit the needs of the places and people around them. Some ancient types of domestic dogs died out, some survived, and some contributed their genes to the development of the many breeds we see around the world today.

Canadian Inuit Dog
For thousands of years, this dog has been the mainstay of transportation for the Inuit peoples living in northwestern Canada.

Malamute
One of the oldest artic sled dog breeds, these dogs were kept by the Mahlemuts, an Inuit tribe.

Carolina Dog
This breed is thought to be a descendant of the ancient dogs who first accompanied humans to North America.

Xoloitzcuintli
The history of this breed is a mystery, but images of similar hairless dogs can be found in Aztec ruins.

Peruvian Inca Orchid
Spanish explorers first saw this ancient breed among the Incan nobility of today's Peru.

Norwegian Buhund
A very old breed, the Buhund originally accompanied hunters and shepherds, and also pulled sleds.

Borzoi
The ancestors of this noble sighthound probably included hunting dogs used by Genghis Khan and the Mongol aristocracy.

Pug
The diminutive Pug was bred from larger dogs at least 2,400 years ago, to be the companion of Buddhist priests.

Irish Wolfhound
These big dogs from Ireland were admired as far away as ancient Rome for their size and nobility.

Shiba Inu
The smallest and oldest of Japan's native breeds, his ancestors lived in mountain regions and hunted a variety of game.

Ibizan Hound
Traders brought the Ibizan Hound to the Balearic Islands thousands of years ago, probably from Egypt.

Greyhound
Ancient carvings from the tomb of Amten in Egypt (built in the early third millennium BCE) show Greyhounds, and the Roman poet Ovid described this breed around the time of Christ.

Basenji
This dog resembles pictures on Egyptian tombs from the Fourth Dynasty. How he made his way to central Africa is a mystery.

Australian Cattle Dog
Crosses between the native dingoes (a wild dog descended from the Asian wolf) and a variety of English working breeds produced these dogs in the 1800s.

How to Use This Book

Welcome to your mutt! This book will teach you how to appreciate your favorite furry friend in a way you've never been able to before: as the sum of his parts. The first thing to do is to learn what to look for, and Part 1 will teach you how to do just that. It may seem odd to divide your dog into body parts such as head, ears, legs, and so forth, but that's the best way to get at your dog's history. When you recognize parts—tails, ears, and so on—that look like your dog, see what type of dog has those same characteristics and what breeds might therefore be in his mix.

Once you're able to recognize all the parts of your dog, you can look through the second part of the book to learn how to apply your newfound talents of identification. Every mutt is, of course, completely individual, but these pages may help you figure out how the whole dog fits together. You should be well-prepared to turn to your own mutt next, capable of reconstructing his heritage!

The sections in Part 1 will give you specific information about the general types of heads, ears, bodies, paws and legs, tails, and coat colors and textures found on dogs.

It's not always easy to understand the special language used to describe canine characteristics, but these visual glossaries will make it all clear.

Here you'll find important information about the characteristics discussed on these pages.

Identifying a Dog's Color and Pattern

Some breeds can be found in a wide range of colors, from white through shades of cream and red to blue, gray, and black. For others, coat color helps define the breed – the Golden Retriever is an excellent example. With a few breeds, the pattern identifies the breed. Think of a Dalmatian and his telltale spots, for instance. Bicolor and tricolor patterns, usually black or brown and white, are especially common in the various scenthounds, but the specific pattern is unique to every individual dog. Other breeds, though, are identified partly by their markings. The Doberman Pinscher and Rottweiler are two examples.

Patched and Brindle

Saddle and Bicolor

More than one pattern can occur on the same dog!

TYPES OF COLORS AND PATTERNS

The colors used to describe dogs frequently embrace a number of different shades. Gold, for example, refers to shades ranging from fawn to tawny, and red can be bright red, golden red, wheaten red, and more. Coat color is not always obvious, either, because dogs can have one color on the outercoat and another on the undercoat. Hairs with bands of color are also a possibility. And different colors can be mixed in the same coat to create spots, speckles, patches, and even complex patterns such as merle and brindle. In addition, there may be much variability within a single breed, and very similar colors and patterns may be shared by many different breeds. As with coat type, color and pattern are usually only helpful in identifying a dog's ancestry when they are considered alongside other features.

Solid

Merle

Badger

Bicolor

Tricolor

Saddle

Black and Tan

Harlequin

Spotted

Patched

Speckled

Brindle

Look for the yellow box to find important distinctions among terms used to describe dogs.

Every dog here also appears on the following page—a gallery of some of the breeds who share each physical characteristic.

Since every mutt is an individual, we decided to give each dog his very own breed name—just for fun!

The big picture! Flip through the book to find a mutt like yours, or just enjoy the parade.

Look in the DOGnosis for the breeds that are likely to be in this mutt's ancestry. The bigger and darker the box, the stronger influence that breed had in this mutt's make-up.

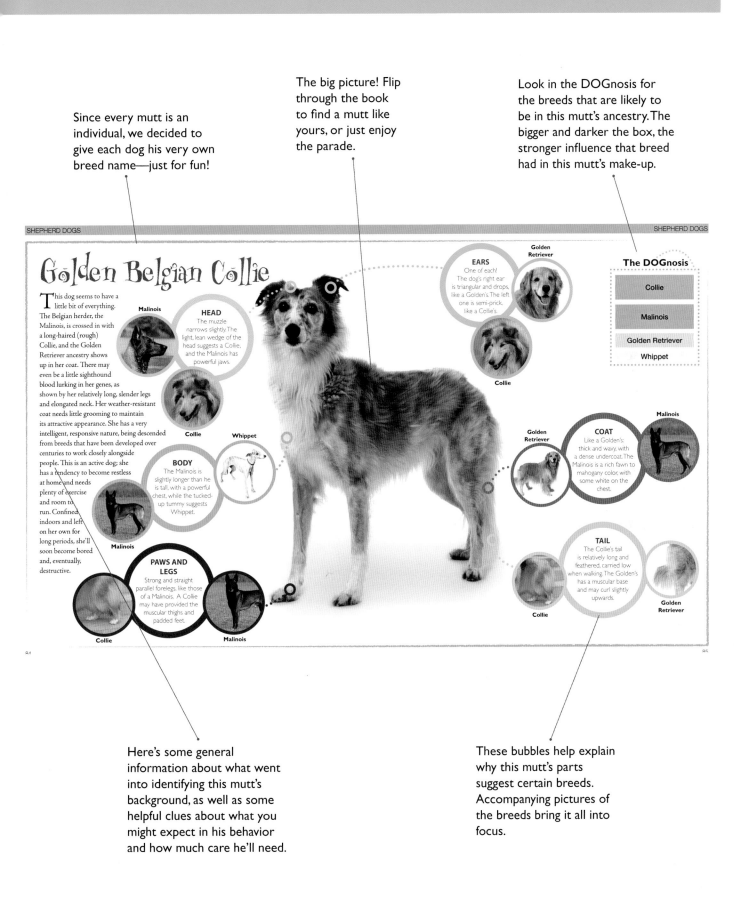

SHEPHERD DOGS

Golden Belgian Collie

This dog seems to have a little bit of everything. The Belgian herder, the Malinois, is crossed in with a long-haired (rough) Collie, and the Golden Retriever ancestry shows up in her coat. There may even be a little sighthound blood lurking in her genes, as shown by her relatively long, slender legs and elongated neck. Her weather-resistant coat needs little grooming to maintain its attractive appearance. She has a very intelligent, responsive nature, being descended from breeds that have been developed over centuries to work closely alongside people. This is an active dog; she has a tendency to become restless at home and needs plenty of exercise and room to run. Confined indoors and left on her own for long periods, she'll soon become bored and, eventually, destructive.

HEAD
The muzzle narrows slightly. The light, lean wedge of the head suggests a Collie, and the Malinois has powerful jaws.

Malinois

Collie

Whippet

BODY
The Malinois is slightly longer than he is tall, with a powerful chest, while the tucked-up tummy suggests Whippet.

Malinois

PAWS AND LEGS
Strong and straight parallel forelegs, like those of a Malinois. A Collie may have provided the muscular thighs and padded feet.

Collie

Malinois

EARS
One of each! The dog's right ear is triangular and drops, like a Golden's. The left one is semi-prick, like a Collie's.

Golden Retriever

Collie

The DOGnosis

Collie

Malinois

Golden Retriever

Whippet

COAT
Like a Golden's: thick and wavy, with a dense undercoat. The Malinois is a rich fawn to mahogany color, with some white on the chest.

Golden Retriever

Malinois

TAIL
The Collie's tail is relatively long and feathered, carried low when walking. The Golden's has a muscular base and may curl slightly upwards.

Collie

Golden Retriever

Here's some general information about what went into identifying this mutt's background, as well as some helpful clues about what you might expect in his behavior and how much care he'll need.

These bubbles help explain why this mutt's parts suggest certain breeds. Accompanying pictures of the breeds bring it all into focus.

Part 1
Identifying a Dog

The best way to identify the breeds that are likely to be in your mutt's make-up is to look at his appearance. Sometimes he'll look a lot like one breed and much less like others, but, because of random inheritances, this can be misleading. Better than trying to assess the whole is to look at individual parts. What you won't find here is a discussion of temperament. Generally speaking, terriers tend to be feisty, tenacious, and curious. The shepherd breeds tend to be easy to train and good with families. The sighthounds are unreliable off leash, might chase other pets, and are independent thinkers. The scenthounds are serious and vocal. The hunting dogs—spaniels, setters, retrievers, and pointers—are active, alert, and also good with families. But these are broad generalities. Each dog is an individual, and that is especially true when it comes to mutts. The best way to know a dog is to meet him—and to ask the shelter workers about him, as well. Never choose a dog on looks alone.

Identifying a Dog's Ear Shape

Wolves have prick ears, which are upright and triangular, and some breeds retain the ear shape of these original canine ancestors. Other breeds have ears that hang down, against the sides of the head. And still others have ears that are somewhere in between. Some dogs' ears hang down when they are relaxed but are raised when they hear interesting sounds. Dogs can also swivel their ears like radar dishes to follow sounds. When you look at your dog's ears, don't just look at the size and shape. It's also important to see where they are located on his head.

TYPES OF EARS

A specific vocabulary has been developed to describe all the different ear types, but since many of these terms are based on everyday objects, it's not hard to figure out their meanings.

Some ear types are associated with a breed type. Hunting dogs, for instance, often have drop ears, which fold over close to the head and hang down, while terriers very frequently have button ears, which are small and fold forward at the tips. However, some terriers have prick ears, which are also characteristic of shepherd dogs, so things are not always perfectly straightforward. Ear shape can also be deceptive in young dogs, because some breeds, such as German Shepherds, have ears that hang down or fold over when they are puppies, but stand upright when they are adults.

Some mutts will have ears that are unique to them—an individual combination that isn't found on any breed. And if you have a particularly furry dog, you may have trouble even finding his ears!

Prick

Drop

Button

Hound

Semi-prick

Tulip

High Set
Ears above a dog's eye level are considered high set.

Rose

Flying

Low Set
Ears that begin below a dog's eye level are low set.

A Gallery of Ears

There are many different ear types, and identifying which one (or ones!) your dog has can help you decipher his ancestry. Use this gallery to help you name your mutt's ears and see which breeds have similar ones, but keep in mind that within each category there are many variations.

PRICK EARS

Australian Cattle Dog

Cairn Terrier

Chihuahua

Norwegian Buhund

DROP EARS

Saluki

Chesapeake Bay Retriever

Cocker Spaniel

Rhodesian Ridgeback

ROSE EARS

Greyhound

Whippet

TULIP EARS

French Bulldog

Corgi

HOUND EARS

Basset Hound

Beagle

Foxhound

Hamiltonstovare

FLYING EARS

American Staffordshire Terrier

SEMI-PRICK EARS

Collie

Lakeland Terrier

BUTTON EARS

Border Terrier

Shar-Pei

Norfolk Terrier

Tibetan Spaniel

Identifying a Dog's Head

Head shapes can vary between extremes, from very narrow and elongated, like a Collie's, to short and round, like a Pug's. As with other body parts, features of a dog's head were developed with specific functions in mind, and therefore can be helpful in determining your mutt's ancestry. For instance, eyes which are placed close together, along with a slender muzzle, suggest a sighthound ancestor—these dogs hunt by tracking their prey visually, and that arrangement gives them great depth perception without obstructing their field of view. Wide, powerful jaws, and the wide skull needed to support them, are characteristic of dogs bred for guarding and similar duties.

TYPES OF HEADS

There are several parts of the head that are used to identify specific head types. The top of the head can be flat or domed, wide or narrow. The cheeks can be prominent or flat. The muzzle can be long or short, blunt or pointed. The flews (lips) can be tight or loose. The eyes can be big or small, set wide apart or close together. The place where the forehead ends and the muzzle begins—called the stop—can be either very pronounced (like a right angle), almost nonexistent, or something in between.

The terms used to describe head shape sometimes refer to other animals, such as foxes or otters. In other cases, they simply describe the head's appearance, as in blocky, wedge-shaped, short, or tapering. Dogs' heads can be described in profile, head-on, or from the top.

Balanced

Blocky

Rectangular

Short

Fox-like

Otter

Tapering

Wedge-shaped

Squared-off Muzzle
The muzzle is strong and ends in a flat plane.

Pointed Muzzle
The muzzle tapers to a point at the nose, like a fox.

A Gallery of Heads

There are many different ways of looking at a dog's head, and several parts of the head can reveal clues about your mutt's ancestry. Use this gallery to help you characterize your mutt's head, but keep in mind that a dog can have a hound muzzle and a hunting dog skull—or any other combination!

BALANCED

Airedale Terrier

Malinois

English Springer Spaniel

Golden Retriever

BLOCKY

American Staffordshire Terrier

Bulldog

Rhodesian Ridgeback

Rottweiler

FOX-LIKE

Finnish Lapphund

Shiba Inu

Keeshond

Pomeranian

OTTER

TAPERING

Border Terrier

Borzoi

Saluki

Whippet

RECTANGULAR

Irish Wolfhound

Scottish Terrier

Soft Coated Wheaten Terrier

Wire Fox Terrier

SHORT

Bulldog

Pug

French Bulldog

Tibetan Spaniel

WEDGE-SHAPED

Finnish Spitz

Collie

Australian Shepherd

Doberman Pinscher

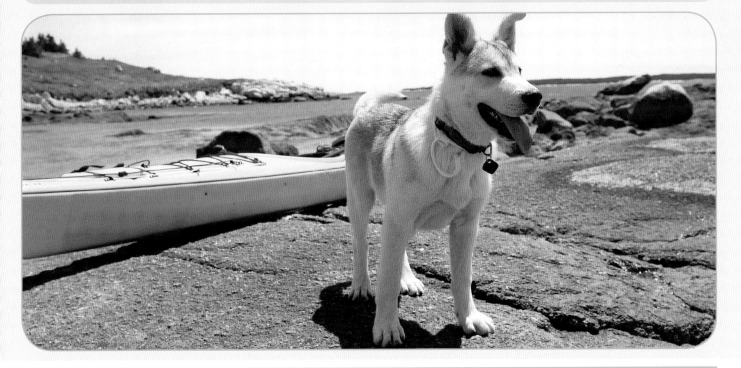

Identifying a Dog's Body Shape

You can pick up important clues to your mutt's origins by assessing her overall body shape. A deep chest, extending down to the level of the elbows, indicates good lung capacity and means this is a dog whose ancestors were designed to run and be active. A more rotund shape is associated with a less athletic lifestyle. A broad chest is a sign of strength, and is characteristic of sled dogs, guard dogs, and other breeds for whom power is important. There are even a few breeds, such as Dachshunds, whose unusual body shape was developed for a very specific purpose—in their case, hunting badgers in underground burrows.

TYPES OF BODIES

When you look at a dog's body in profile, it has an overall shape, composed of several important characteristics. For example, it may be square, rectangular, or long, and, depending on the length of the legs, the dog may be tall or short. The underside may curve up under the tummy—called a tuck-up. The chest may curve down from the body. The topline may be level, slope towards the rump, or dip a bit at the top of the shoulders. Head-on, the body might be broad or lithe, massive and blocky, or light and elegant. Overall body type certainly tells you what work this dog was bred to do. When you look at your dog, ask yourself: Does this look like the body of a runner, a guardian, a hunter, or simply a companion?

Deep Chest

Massive/blocky

Broad Chest

Lithe

Tall

Short

Square

Long

Level Topline
The back is perfectly straight and level.

Sloping Topline
This topline slopes away at the rump.

Rectangular

Tuck-up

A Gallery of Body Shapes

There are many different body types, and identifying which one your dog has can help you understand what kind of job your dog was meant to do. Use this gallery to help you name your mutt's body type and see which breeds look similar, but keep in mind that within each category there are many variations.

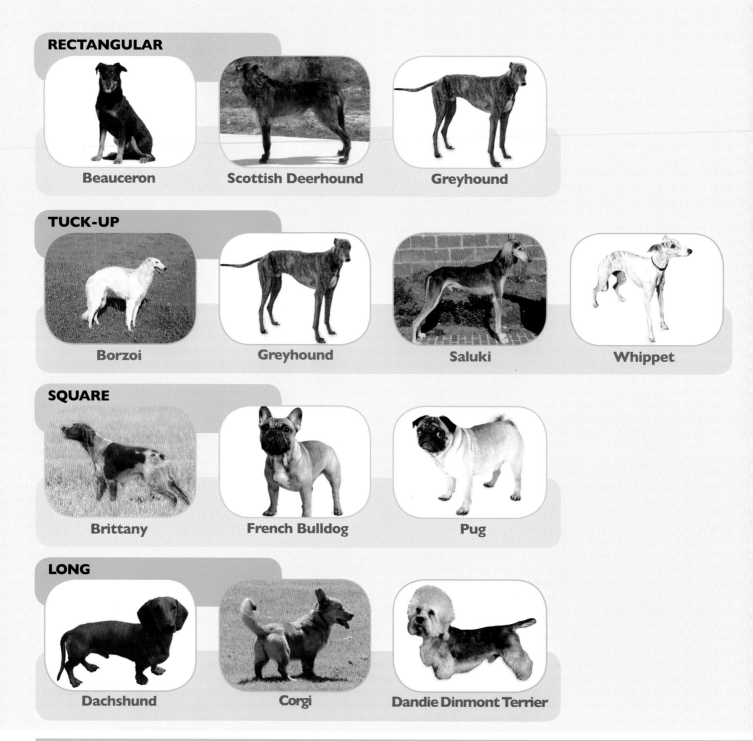

RECTANGULAR

Beauceron

Scottish Deerhound

Greyhound

TUCK-UP

Borzoi

Greyhound

Saluki

Whippet

SQUARE

Brittany

French Bulldog

Pug

LONG

Dachshund

Corgi

Dandie Dinmont Terrier

DEEP CHEST

Pointer

Doberman Pinscher

Beauceron

Rhodesian Ridgeback

BROAD CHEST

Bulldog

Malamute

Labrador Retriever

Rottweiler

SHORT

Cairn Terrier

Yorkshire Terrier

TALL

Great Dane

Irish Wolfhound

MASSIVE/BLOCKY

American Staffordshire Terrier

Bulldog

Bullmastiff

Shar-Pei

LITHE

Ibizan Hound

Saluki

Whippet

Identifying a Dog's Coat

Long, short, soft, or wiry—there are a number of different possible combinations for coats. There are even a few breeds with very little hair at all. Coat type sometimes tells you a lot—as with terriers, many of whom have distinctive wiry coats, and northern breeds, who have thick, plush double coats. But sometimes coat type can be deceptive, because a few breeds, such as the Dachshund, have been developed in longhaired, shorthaired, and wirecoated variations. It's also true that a mutt may show the coat characteristics of several of his ancestors.

Double Coat
Most dogs have a short, soft undercoat and a longer outercoat.

Single Coat
Some breeds have just a single, short coat.

TYPES OF COATS

While you can often assess the coat texture simply from a dog's appearance, you may need to part the fur on some dogs to see whether, for example, there is a dense undercoat close to the skin. Coat length is often a clue to ancestry, but the length of the coat is not necessarily consistent over the entire body. The fur is often shorter on the face than elsewhere, and sometimes longer on the legs and tail (called feathering). The coat contributes greatly to the overall look of the dog, and often we are tempted to choose a dog on looks alone. But in the long run, personality is far more important than looks when you're considering a new pet.

Bristle

Close

Single

Double

Crinkly

Curly

Smooth

Glossy

Stand-off

Thick

Wire

A Gallery of Coats

We tend to think of canine coats as just short or long, but there are many variations on that theme. Identifying your dog's coat type will tell you something about the part of the world he came from and the work he was bred to do. Use this gallery to help you name your mutt's coat type and find breeds with a similar coat. Remember, however, that there is a lot of variability in each category.

BRISTLE

Shar-Pei

Shiba Inu

CRINKLY

Wire Fox Terrier

Airedale Terrier

CLOSE

American Staffordshire Terrier

Australian Cattle Dog

Greyhound

Whippet

CURLY

Irish Water Spaniel

Standard Poodle

DOUBLE

Akita

Bearded Collie

GLOSSY

Chihuahua

Dalmatian

Flat-Coated Retriever

Manchester Terrier

SINGLE

Papillon

Miniature Pinscher

Weimaraner

Standard Poodle

SMOOTH

Basset Hound

Beagle

Boxer

Doberman Pinscher

STAND-OFF

Norweigan Elkhound

Keeshond

Pomeranian

Shiba Inu

THICK

Affenpinscher

Australian Shepherd

Labrador Retriever

Siberian Husky

WIRE

Irish Terrier

Norfolk Terrier

Border Terrier

Scottish Deerhound

Identifying a Dog's Color and Pattern

S ome breeds can be found in a wide range of colors, from white through shades of cream and red to blue, gray, and black. For others, coat color helps define the breed—the Golden Retriever is an excellent example. With a few breeds, the pattern identifies the breed. Think of a Dalmatian and his telltale spots, for instance. Bicolor and tricolor patterns, usually black or brown and white, are especially common in the various scenthounds, but the specific pattern is unique to every individual dog. Other breeds, though, are identified partly by their markings. The Doberman Pinscher and Rottweiler are two examples.

Patched and Brindle

Saddle and Bicolor

More than one pattern can occur on the same dog!

TYPES OF COLORS AND PATTERNS

The colors used to describe dogs frequently embrace a number of different shades. Gold, for example, refers to shades ranging from fawn to tawny, and red can be bright red, golden red, wheaten red, and more. Coat color is not always obvious, either, because dogs can have one color on the outercoat and another on the undercoat. Hairs with bands of color are also a possibility. And different colors can be mixed in the same coat to create spots, speckles, patches, and even complex patterns such as merle and brindle. In addition, there may be much variability within a single breed, and very similar colors and patterns may be shared by many different breeds. As with coat type, color and pattern are usually only helpful in identifying a dog's ancestry when they are considered alongside other features.

Solid   Merle   Badger   Bicolor

Tricolor   Saddle   Black and Tan   Harlequin

Spotted   Patched   Speckled   Brindle

A Gallery of Colors and Patterns

Dogs come in an almost infinite array of colors and patterns. Sometimes they tell us a great deal about a mutt's ancestry, but sometimes they just help narrow things down a bit or even tell us almost nothing.

This gallery will help you name your mutt's pattern and show you which breeds have a similar look. Colors and patterns are some of the trickiest and most variable of features, so don't judge your dog by his coat alone!

MERLE

Australian Cattle Dog

BADGER

Petit Basset Griffon Vendeen

SOLID

Affenpinscher

Flat-Coated Retriever

Irish Terrier

Vizsla

BICOLOR

Border Collie

Finnish Lapphund

Australian Terrier

Bearded Collie

TRICOLOR

Basset Hound

Jack Russell Terrier

Greater Swiss Mountain Dog

Corgi

SADDLE

Airedale Terrier

German Shepherd

Welsh Terrier

HARLEQUIN

Great Dane

BLACK AND TAN

Beauceron

Manchester Terrier

Rottweiler

Doberman Pinscher

PATCHED

Ibizan Hound

Papillon

Cavalier King Charles Spaniel

Brittany

SPECKLED

German Shorthaired Pointer

English Setter

English Springer Spaniel

SPOTTED

Dalmatian

BRINDLE

Whippet

Greyhound

Identifying a Dog's Tail

All dogs use their tails to communicate their moods, and the special signals they send are the same for all types of dogs. But the shape and position of the tail can vary a great deal among the breeds. For example, hounds who hunt in packs, such as Beagles and Foxhounds, have straight tails that they carry upright, like a flag. In contrast, sighthounds carry their tails low, with either a gentle curve at the end or right between their legs. Most terriers have upright tails set high on their backs.

High Set
A tail that seems to be a natural extension of the topline is high set.

Low Set
A tail that begins below the topline is low set.

TYPES OF TAILS

The shape of the tail, its length, and the way it is held will influence what it's called—and will give you a clue to your dog's heritage. The brush tail, for example, describes a heavily-furred tail that is carried close to the ground. A sickle tail curves forward over the back, and when you combine the two, you have a brush sickle tail—as on a Siberian Husky. Screw tails are short with a twist in them, like a Pug's, while gay tails are held vertically, like a Wire Fox Terrier's. There are a few breeds, such as the Cardigan Welsh Corgi, which have very short bobtails; this is a natural genetic variation. Dogs with very short tails have been known to wag their whole back end when they're excited!

Whip

Tufted

Plume

Sabre

Brush

Curled

Snap

Sword

Gay

Otter

Tapering

A Gallery of Tails

There are many different types of tails, and sometimes more than one descriptive word will apply to the same tail. Use this gallery to help you name your mutt's tail type and see which breeds have similar tails. As always, there are many variations, and your mutt may have a tail all his own!

BRUSH

Siberian Husky

Finnish Spitz

OTTER

Chesapeake Bay Retriever

Labrador Retriever

CURLED

Akita

Pug

SWORD

American Staffordshire Terrier

Great Dane

Greater Swiss Mountain Dog

Pointer

SNAP

Malamute

Pomeranian

TUFTED

Standard Poodle

Miniature Poodle

GAY

Cavalier King Charles Spaniel

Beagle

German Shorthaired Pointer

Wire Fox Terrier

TAPERING

Dachshund

Manchester Terrier

Border Terrier

SABRE

German Shepherd

Petit Basset Griffon Vendeen

PLUME

Borzoi

Saluki

Tervuren

WHIP

Whippet

Ibizan Hound

Identifying a Dog's Paws and Legs

Long
Not all long-legged
dogs are tall!

Short
Not all short-legged
dogs are tiny!

In addition to looking at the length and thickness of a dog's legs, the angle at which they join the body tells us a lot about the dog's athletic ability. The position of the legs is also influenced by the body shape; a broad-chested dog, for instance, is likely to have wide-set limbs. The shape of the paws also helps indicate what type of activity the dog was bred for. Northern breeds have thick, hard footpads, necessary for running on hard earth and snow, while webbing between the toes is common in breeds that work in water, such as Labrador Retrievers.

TYPES OF PAWS AND LEGS

It's not just the length of a mutt's legs that is significant in terms of determining her possible ancestry, but also the shape. In some breeds, such as Basset Hounds and Bulldogs, the front legs are turned outwards. In other breeds, including many terriers, the front legs are perfectly straight, have a crisp bend at the wrist, and end in paws that point straight ahead. There are a number of different paw shapes too; rounder paws provide strength and stability, while hare-shaped paws (long and narrow) are built for speed and typify some of the faster breeds (although many toy breeds have them too). Powerful muscles on the back legs suggest an ancestor bred for strength or speed, but these should be considered in combination with the mutt's general body shape.

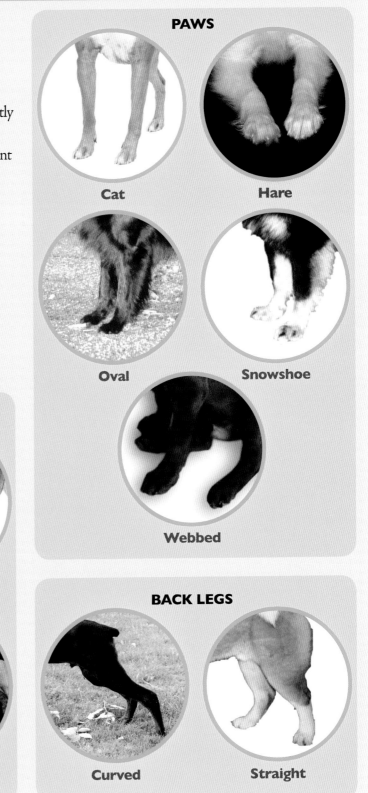

PAWS

Cat

Hare

Oval

Snowshoe

Webbed

FRONT LEGS

Straight

Bowed

Bent (at wrist)

Wide-set

BACK LEGS

Curved

Straight

A Gallery of Paws and Legs

There are more types of paws and legs than you might think, and identifying which ones your dog has can give you clues to her background. Use this gallery to help you name your mutt's paws and legs and see which breeds are similar, but keep in mind that every category has many variations.

PAWS

CAT

Boxer

Miniature Pinscher

Cocker Spaniel

Beagle

HARE

Borzoi

Papillon

OVAL

Bearded Collie

Flat-Coated Retriever

SNOWSHOE

Finnish Lapphund

Malamute

Norwegian Elkhound

Siberian Husky

WEBBED

Chesapeake Bay Retriever

Labrador Retriever

BACK LEGS

CURVED

Brittany

Doberman Pinscher

STRAIGHT

Akita

Cairn Terrier

Finnish Lapphund

Smooth Fox Terrier

FRONT LEGS

STRAIGHT

English Springer Spaniel

Manchester Terrier

BOWED

Bulldog

Pug

BENT (AT WRIST)

Basset Hound

Dachshund

WIDE-SET

Bullmastiff

Great Dane

Part 2

David Alderton Identifies the Mutts

The best start to determining the likely origins of a mutt is to first consider his size and body shape. This will give you an initial overall impression of what kind of dog he is. You can then begin to look more carefully at individual aspects of his appearance—head shape, paws and legs, tail, and so forth—in search of further clues about his ancestry. And do not forget that the dog's temperament and behavior may provide you with additional insights. Even with all of this, though, figuring out a mutt's heritage is basically a series of educated guesses. But the effort will certainly teach you a lot about your dog!

Terrier Types

Affencairn

Cairn Terrier

Clearly descended from terrier stock, this is a lively dog who would enjoy living in a suburban home with a backyard and a park nearby for walks, but he would be equally at home in a more rural environment. His coat care is fairly straightforward, since, like most terriers, it is weather-resistant and needs relatively little grooming. In fact, the slightly unkempt appearance adds to his charm. He may, however, benefit from having his coat trimmed back every two or three months. If you're not ready to do that yourself, you may need to take him to a groomer. It is also important to make sure the longer hair around his mouth does not become soiled with food and dirt. You may need to wipe his beard every day, or he'll end up smelling unpleasant.

BODY

The powerful, rectangular body suggests the Cairn Terrier, which has a level back and deep ribs, or Australian Terrier, with his low-reaching chest.

Australian Terrier

Cairn Terrier

COAT

The double coat, found on the Cairn Terrier and Affenpinscher, provides good protection against the elements.

Affenpinscher

PAWS AND LEGS

The overall stocky appearance and short legs are found in Cairn Terriers, whose front feet are slightly bigger than their back feet, and Affenpinschers, which have tight, round feet.

Cairn Terrier

Affenpinscher

EARS

Pointed, well-spaced ears are a balance between the Scottish Terrier, which has bigger ears, and the Australian Terrier, whose ears are smaller.

Scottish Terrier

Australian Terrier

TheDOGnosis

Cairn Terrier
Affenpinscher
Scottish Terrier
Australian Terrier

Cairn Terrier

HEAD

The powerful, square muzzle is most likely from the Cairn Terrier, and the abundant mustache and beard is all Affenpinscher.

Affenpinscher

Smooth Pitfoxstaffie

EARS
Small, located on the top of the skull, and tipped over.

Smooth Fox Terrier

This dog is still growing up, but he is clearly a character. He also has the potential to become a difficult dog without adequate training, being quite strong-willed by nature. He is a terrier and is descended from the tough guys of the terrier group: most likely the American Staffordshire Terrier and the Pit Bull. He is also likely to be rather territorial, and needs socializing with other dogs from an early age. Otherwise, he will not play well with others—especially those who do not recognize his tough-guy nature. On the other hand, the fearsome reputation of the Pit Bull breeds is not entirely justified. These dogs can be trained well, and a number are used in hospital visiting programs and other projects where they have close contact with strangers. Early socialization will help, as will neutering him.

Pit Bull

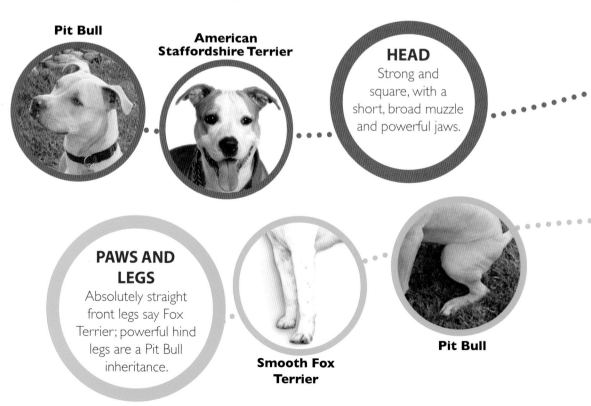

Pit Bull

American Staffordshire Terrier

HEAD
Strong and square, with a short, broad muzzle and powerful jaws.

PAWS AND LEGS
Absolutely straight front legs say Fox Terrier; powerful hind legs are a Pit Bull inheritance.

Smooth Fox Terrier

Pit Bull

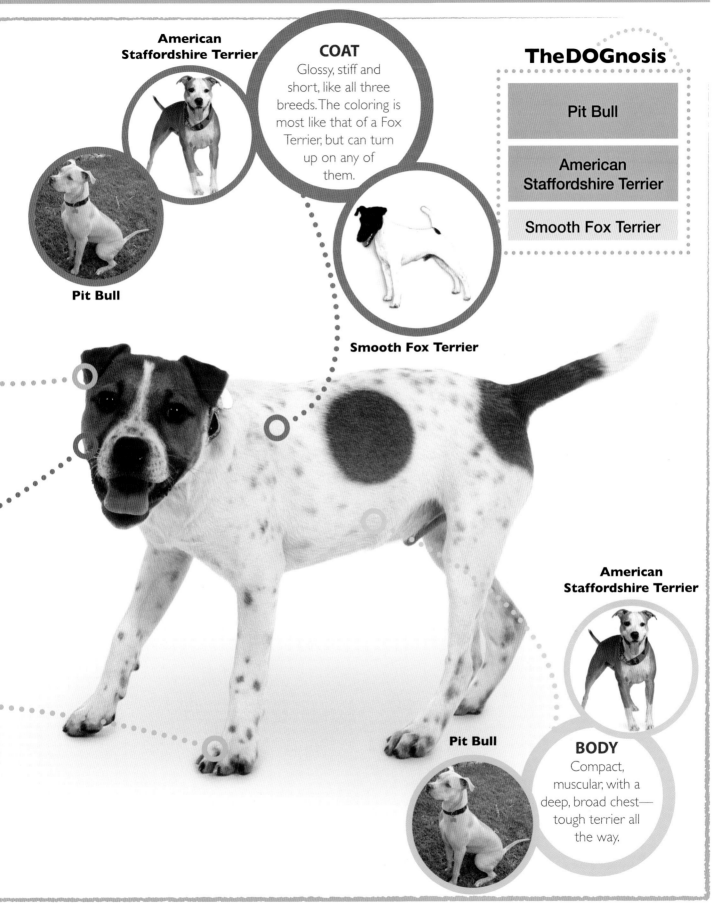

American Staffordshire Terrier

Pit Bull

COAT
Glossy, stiff and short, like all three breeds. The coloring is most like that of a Fox Terrier, but can turn up on any of them.

Smooth Fox Terrier

TheDOGnosis

Pit Bull

American Staffordshire Terrier

Smooth Fox Terrier

American Staffordshire Terrier

Pit Bull

BODY
Compact, muscular, with a deep, broad chest—tough terrier all the way.

WheatLake Terrier

This dog has an alert, curious nature with an independent streak that can hamper his training. He likes people but tends not to be very friendly toward other dogs. These traits give us a clue to his ancestry as a cross-bred terrier—which helps explain his tousled coat, the shape of his ears, and the way he holds his tail. His coloration suggests that he has some Soft Coated Wheaten Terrier in his background; the breed has a softer coat than most terriers, and it is the color of ripening wheat. The other terriers in his background give this dog his long legs, fuzzy face, and mischievous nature.

Irish Terrier

EARS
Set high and wide on the head, V-shaped, and folded forward.

Soft Coated Wheaten Terrier

Lakeland Terrier

HEAD
Rectangular, with a long, powerful muzzle and a broad nose.

Wire Fox Terrier

Lakeland Terrier

COAT
A wiry look that is actually soft to the touch, plus that rich yellowish-gold, says Soft Coated Wheaten. But the bushy face suggests the Lakeland.

Soft Coated Wheaten Terrier

PAWS AND LEGS
The beautiful, straight front legs are found on all of these terriers, while the round, compact feet are from the Wire Fox.

Lakeland Terrier

Irish Terrier

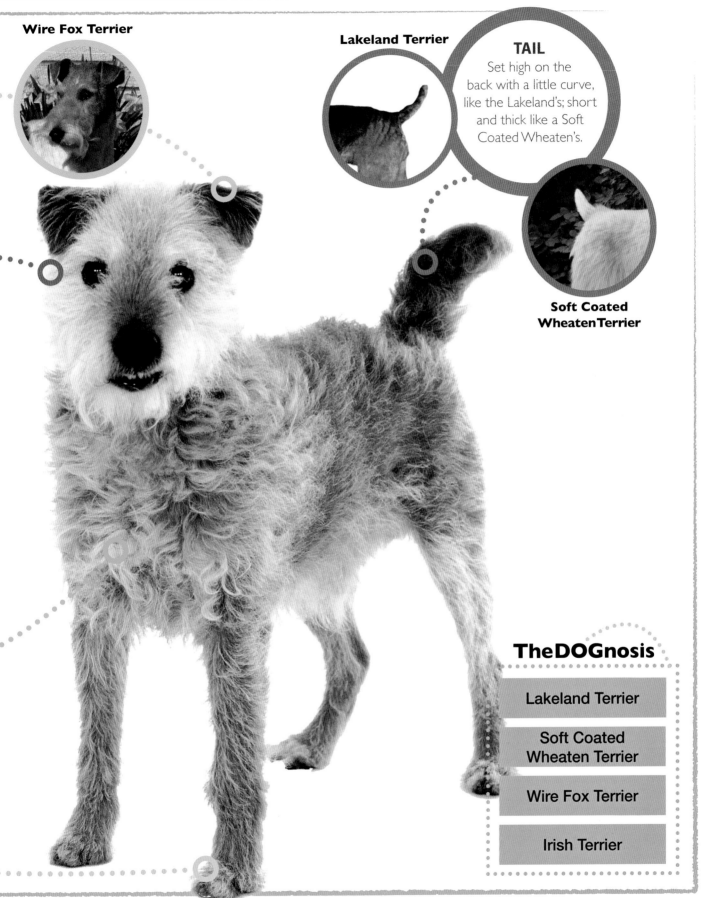

Wire Fox Terrier

Lakeland Terrier

TAIL
Set high on the back with a little curve, like the Lakeland's; short and thick like a Soft Coated Wheaten's.

Soft Coated Wheaten Terrier

TheDOGnosis

Lakeland Terrier
Soft Coated Wheaten Terrier
Wire Fox Terrier
Irish Terrier

Northern Manfolk Terrier

There is no doubt that this dog is descended, in part, from one of the northern breeds (also known as Spitz breeds), probably a Shiba Inu or a Finnish Spitz (depending on where she lives). She has some of the typical characteristics of those breeds, including a tail that curves over her back and a pointed, fox-like face. However, her folded-over ears and scruffy coat suggest some terrier in her make-up. So we could say this dog is a northern breed at both ends and a terrier in the middle. Certainly, she is responsive and friendly, although she can be noisy—a reflection of both her northern heritage and the instinctive alertness of a terrier.

Finnish Spitz

HEAD
Tapers to a triangle, with a pointy muzzle and dark eyes.

Shiba Inu

Smooth Fox Terrier

Norfolk Terrier

EARS
Small and set well-back on the head, with dropped tips.

COAT
The color is more like that of a Shiba or a Finnish Spitz, but the texture is wiry like a terrier's.

Finnish Spitz

Shiba Inu

Norfolk Terrier

PAWS AND LEGS
Short straight legs, with compact, rounded feet—traits of both the Manchester and the Smooth Fox Terriers.

Manchester Terrier

Smooth Fox Terrier

TAIL
The short tail has some feathering on the underside and curls forward; it looks a lot like the tails of the northern breeds.

Finnish Spitz

Shiba Inu

TheDOGnosis

Finnish Spitz/Shiba Inu

Norfolk Terrier

Manchester Terrier

Smooth Fox Terrier

Dandie Border Scottie

A dog with an unmistakable terrier profile, his rather long face suggests a Scottish Terrier—but only in part. A little Dandie Dinmont Terrier in his ancestry would help to explain the folded ears, as well as the tuft on the top of his head. His coloration is also faintly reminiscent of a Dandie Dinmont —a mixture sometimes described as "pepper-and-salt" —and his long, low body could be Cairn Terrier or more Dandie. Ever-alert and quite strong-willed (like all terriers), he loves investigating every hole in the ground. He is not deterred by bad weather, either, being well-protected from the elements by his wiry double coat.

BODY
Broad and close to the ground, like both the Dandie and Cairn, and long like a Dandie.

Dandie Dinmont Terrier

Cairn Terrier

Border Terrier

Scottish Terrier

TAIL
Short and thick, tapering to a point.

PAWS AND LEGS
Short, straight legs suggest Dandie Dinmont, with the front feet bigger than the hind feet, as on a Border Terrier.

Dandie Dinmont Terrier

Border Terrier

HEAD
Broad at the top of the skull, with a short, wide muzzle.

Scottish Terrier

Dandie Dinmont Terrier

COAT
Medium length and wiry like a Cairn; pepper-and-salt, hard-and-soft like a Dandie.

Cairn Terrier

Dandie Dinmont Terrier

TheDOGnosis

Scottish Terrier

Dandie Dinmont Terrier

Border Terrier

Cairn Terrier

Norcairnshire Terrier

His broad face, folded ears, short legs, and a coat that is longer over the shoulders than on the body are all clues that point to a Norfolk Terrier ancestor. It's likely that the Border Terrier played a part too, with that large, round face. His coat is much less wiry than that of most terriers, suggesting there might be a little bit of Yorkie lurking here too. He is an active dog, keen to go out even when the weather is bad, trotting along rather than running—but certainly never walking slowly with those short legs. His coat is easy to keep clean; any dirt that sticks to it will soon dry and can then be easily brushed out.

HEAD
Broad and flat on top indicate Norfolk and Border Terriers, and the compact muzzle is Border all the way. The big, round eyes are like a Yorkie's.

Yorkshire Terrier

Border Terrier

Norfolk Terrier

BODY
Longer than he is tall, like a Norfolk, with a deep chest like a Cairn.

Cairn Terrier

Norfolk Terrier

COAT
Scruffy and reddish, like a typical Norfolk, but not harsh to the touch, like a Yorkie.

Yorkshire Terrier

PAWS AND LEGS
Short, with the front legs angled slightly forward like a Cairn's and well-angled at the rear, like a Norfolk's.

Norfolk Terrier

Cairn Terrier

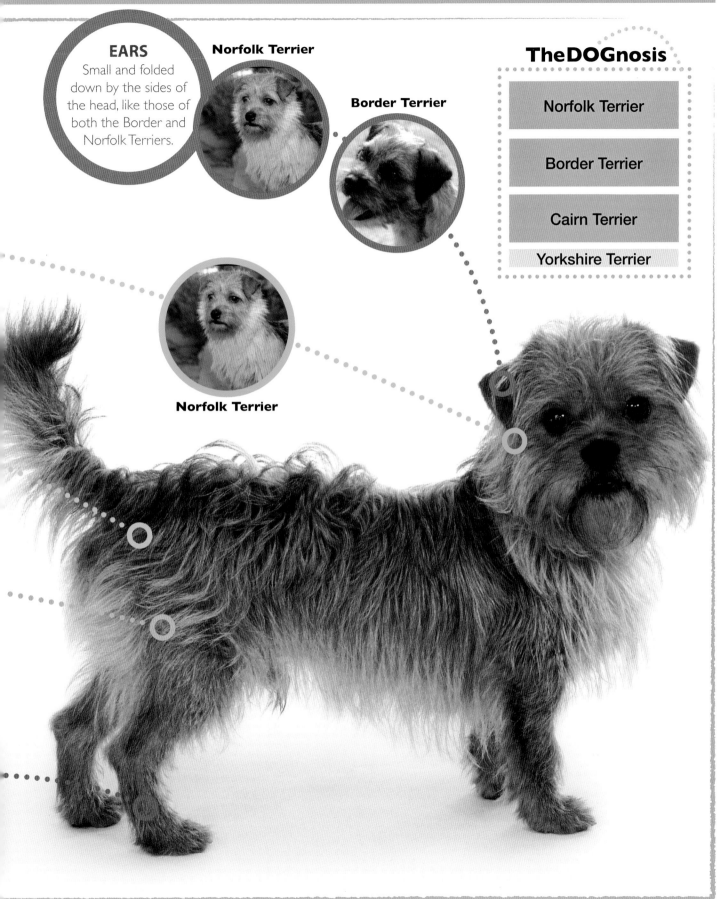

EARS
Small and folded down by the sides of the head, like those of both the Border and Norfolk Terriers.

Norfolk Terrier

Border Terrier

Norfolk Terrier

TheDOGnosis

Norfolk Terrier

Border Terrier

Cairn Terrier

Yorkshire Terrier

Welman Terrier

There is little doubt that this dog is another descendant of terrier stock. In the past, there was a different terrier type for almost every town and village. But nowadays there's a lot of intermingling. And all terriers everywhere have certain characteristics that can be recognized right away: the squarish muzzle with a beard underneath, the wiry coat, the strong back and chest, the tail that's short but not stubby. This lively terrier is still young, but you can see even now that she will develop into a solidly built adult. Her intense, curious expression is also pure terrier. Tenacious and energetic, this dog needs a lot of activity to keep her from becoming yappy and destructive, and will love poking her nose into every available hole.

HEAD
The head narrows slightly (like a Manchester's) down to the square muzzle (like a Welsh Terrier's).

Manchester Terrier

Welsh Terrier

COAT
Wiry and thick at the beard and chest, like the Welsh Terrier. Her color suggests the black and tan of the Manchester.

Manchester Terrier

Welsh Terrier

Manchester Terrier

Airedale Terrier

PAWS AND LEGS
Long, strong, straight legs are from the Manchester, and her height suggests some Airedale.

Welsh Terrier

EARS
Small and folded forward, like those of so many terriers.

Wire Fox Terrier

Airedale Terrier

TheDOGnosis

Welsh Terrier

Manchester Terrier

Wire Fox Terrier

Airedale Terrier

Manchester Terrier

BODY
The Manchester is a bit more sleek and slender than the typical terrier, while the length suggests an Airedale.

Airedale Terrier

Bullbox Terrier

Any of the Bulldog breeds, which were originally developed to fight, or Mastiff breeds, which were bred to be fearsome guardians, could be part of this dog's heritage—especially as these dogs have been crossbred since the late 1700s. Don't believe the fearsome reputation these dogs have; they're not hard to train and will be lively companions. They'll thrive in a home with teenagers who have similar high energy levels and enjoy playing with them. Such dogs are quite territorial by nature, though, and are alert to the presence of strangers. Training is important to keep their assertive side in check.

EARS
Button ears, set high on the head and framing the face.

Boxer

Bullmastiff

BODY
Well-muscled, with a big, broad chest like a Bulldog. Square profile like a Boxer and a Pit Bull.

Pit Bull

Boxer

COAT
Sleek, short, and smooth, with almost no undercoat. The white with tan patches also suggest a bit of the bull.

Pit Bull

Bulldog

PAWS AND LEGS
Strong legs and big, powerful paws, like the Pit Bull's and Bulldog's. Well-muscled, curving thighs and straight front legs, like the Boxer's.

Boxer

Pit Bull

Bulldog

HEAD
Broad overall, with a short, wide muzzle and loose lips.

Pit Bull

Bullmastiff

Bulldog

TheDOGnosis

Pit Bull

Boxer

Bullmastiff

Bulldog

Lakelsh Foxder Terrier

This very unusual terrier was born without ears, which makes him one dog in a million ... or more! It has not affected his hearing, though. The absence of ears is the result of a genetic quirk. Although some breeds have much smaller ears than others, no external ear flaps at all is not a feature of any breed. With or without the ears, though, this dog is clearly a terrier. You can see it in his coat, his overall shape, and even his grizzled little beard, not to mention his active and curious nature. This boy was born in Wales, so the Welsh Terrier is likely part of his ancestry. But you can see other influences, as well.

Border Terrier

HEAD

Quite broad and short says Border Terrier, but he has a bit of a break between the forehead and the start of the muzzle, like both the Border and Fox Terriers.

Welsh Terrier

TAIL

Short, positioned high on the back, and held straight up, like those of so many terrier breeds.

Lakeland Terrier

COAT

The wiry texture and the colors—black saddle on a tan background—suggest both the Lakeland and Welsh Terriers.

Welsh Terrier

Lakeland Terrier

PAWS AND LEGS

The feet are round, compact, and small like the Fox Terrier's, with relatively short thighs on the rear legs, like the Welsh Terrier's.

Welsh Terrier

Wire Fox Terrier

Wire Fox Terrier

Welsh Terrier

BODY
Compact and sturdy like the Welsh Terrier, with a steep angle to his profile underneath, like the Lakeland.

Lakeland Terrier

The DOGnosis

Welsh Terrier

Lakeland Terrier

Wire Fox Terrier

Border Terrier

Irish Aire Terrier

One look at this dog and you know he's a terrier. It's the hard, wiry coat and beard on the muzzle that give it away. A rather tall terrier, in fact, which suggests an Airedale or Irish Terrier. But there's more to this boy, and his coloring suggests Lakeland or Welsh Terrier in his background, as well. He displays distinct terrier-like behavior, too, which means he likes to explore and run and chase. He has plenty of energy, and those long legs help him move much faster than most terriers. He is bold by nature, and will make a good guardian around the home.

HEAD
The ears are V-shaped and fold down away from the head, like all terrier breeds. The flat skull, the small break between the muzzle and the eyes, and the dark, intense eyes, suggest Irish Terrier. The Lakeland's skull is also flat on top, with a strong muzzle.

Airedale Terrier

TAIL
The root of the tail is set high on the back, and is short, thick, and carried up.

Lakeland Terrier

BODY
This dog is tall, like both the Irish and Airedale Terriers. Like the Irish, he also has long shoulders and a chest that is neither deep nor wide.

Airedale Terrier

Irish Terrier

PAWS AND LEGS
Moderately long legs and strong hindquarters with no droop are from the Airedale, and the small, round feet with thick black nails are from the Welsh Terrier.

Airedale Terrier

Welsh Terrier

Irish Terrier

Lakeland Terrier

Welsh Terrier

Airedale Terrier

Lakeland Terrier

COAT
The coat texture is all terrier, and the colors—tan with a black saddle—are common to Airedale, Welsh, and Lakeland Terriers.

TheDOGnosis

Airedale Terrier

Irish Terrier

Lakeland Terrier

Welsh Terrier

Bullman Box Terrier

This dog's stocky appearance is due to her Bull Terrier genes, but a past cross with a Manchester Terrier might have been responsible for narrowing her face and extending the length of her muzzle. She is not very keen on running, with her body frame being better-suited to ambling along. As a result, it is important to keep a check on her weight to ensure that she does not pile on the pounds. She's a loyal companion, but can be rather short-tempered with other dogs, especially those who just run up to her. It's probably best to keep her on a leash in the park.

Manchester Terrier

HEAD
The broad skull with a short muzzle suggests Pit Bull, but the fact that the head is wedge-shaped and relatively long says Manchester Terrier.

Pit Bull

Manchester Terrier

American Staffordshire Terrier

EARS
These ears are halfway between the prick ears of the Manchester Terrier and the flying ears of the American Staffordshire Terrier.

TheDOGnosis

Pit Bull

American Staffordshire Terrier

Manchester Terrier

Boxer

Boxer

BODY
This stocky, compact, well-muscled body with a wide back and a broad, deep chest, is typical of the Bull Terrier breeds.

Pit Bull

COAT
Smooth and glossy, short and sleek, and contoured to her curves, like all the breeds in our mix.

Pit Bull

Manchester Terrier

American Staffordshire Terrier

American Staffordshire Terrier

Manchester Terrier

PAWS AND LEGS
Relatively slim and straight front legs are like the Manchester's, the well-muscled hindquarters are from the American Staffordshire Terrier, and the round, small feet are like the Boxer's.

Boxer

American Staffordshire Terrier

Miniature Vizdale

The beautiful color and rough coat tell us this is a tall terrier with some hunting dog mixed in—perhaps the Vizsla. This is an energetic, exuberant dog with an inquisitive nature. Although some areas of his coat are longer than others, grooming is quite straightforward—just brush and go. Particular attention does need to be paid to the longer hair around his mouth, though. As with all terriers, the "beard" can become soiled and matted by food. It's a good idea to wipe your terrier's face with a clean cloth every day after he eats. This is especially true if he eats wet food of any kind.

Border Terrier

HEAD
The head is strong and rectangular, and flat on the top of the skull, like a Miniature Schnauzer's. The Border Terrier has a round muzzle with a distinctive break between the forehead and the muzzle.

Miniature Schnauzer

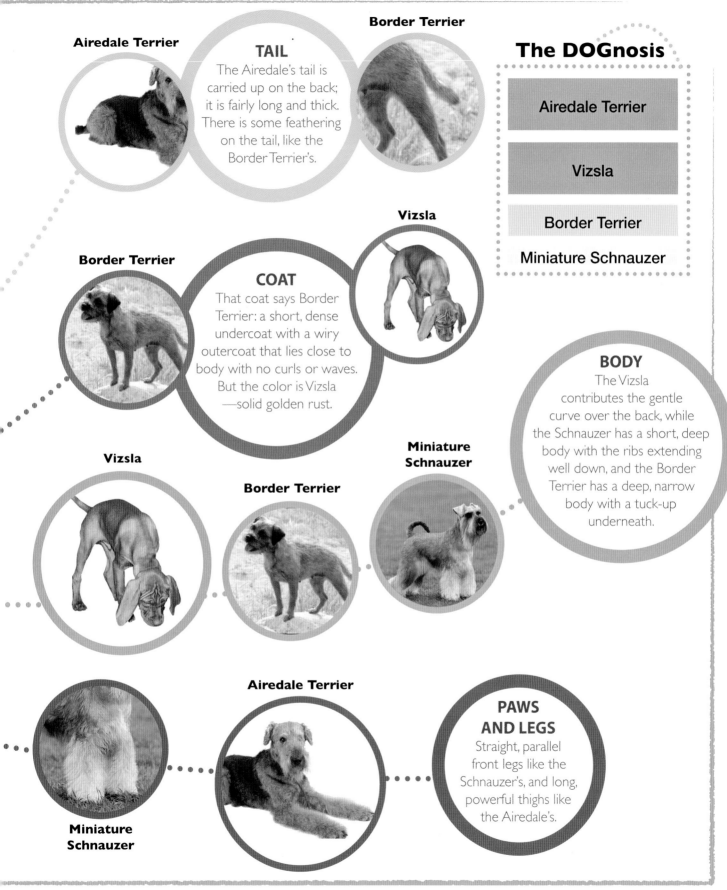

Airedale Terrier

Border Terrier

TAIL
The Airedale's tail is carried up on the back; it is fairly long and thick. There is some feathering on the tail, like the Border Terrier's.

The DOGnosis

Airedale Terrier

Vizsla

Border Terrier

Miniature Schnauzer

Vizsla

Border Terrier

COAT
That coat says Border Terrier: a short, dense undercoat with a wiry outercoat that lies close to body with no curls or waves. But the color is Vizsla —solid golden rust.

BODY
The Vizsla contributes the gentle curve over the back, while the Schnauzer has a short, deep body with the ribs extending well down, and the Border Terrier has a deep, narrow body with a tuck-up underneath.

Vizsla

Border Terrier

Miniature Schnauzer

Miniature Schnauzer

Airedale Terrier

PAWS AND LEGS
Straight, parallel front legs like the Schnauzer's, and long, powerful thighs like the Airedale's.

73

Great Bullbox Terrier

Dogs of this type often used to be known as Bull and Terrier dogs. They're the other kind of terriers—the ones with the wide, blocky heads and short coats, rather than the wiry, scruffy sort. The brindle pattern comes from a working dog heritage, though. This is a powerfully built, energetic dog. He'll need to be well-trained to get all that energy under control. Working dogs need work to do; he is a dog who must have plenty of toys around to keep him occupied. He may also be wary around other dogs—training will help with that, too.

EARS
This is a combination of the American Staffordshire Terrier's ears, which are set high and held out, and the Great Dane's ears, also high set, of medium thickness and size, and folded forward.

Great Dane

American Staffordshire Terrier

Great Dane

COAT
The coat is short, close, thick, glossy, and stiff, like those of all our breeds. The brindle and white could be Boxer, Bullmastiff, or Great Dane.

Bullmastiff

Boxer

Boxer

BODY
The look of overall strength and the muscular, slightly arched neck come from the American Staffordshire Terrier, while the Boxer brings a touch of lightness to the body, along with a deep chest and a moderate tuck-up at the tummy.

American Staffordshire Terrier

PAWS AND LEGS
The American Staffordshire Terrier's straight front legs and large bones combine here with the Boxer's broad, curved thighs.

American Staffordshire Terrier

Boxer

American
Staffordshire Terrier

HEAD

The American
Staffordshire Terrier has
a broad skull and a medium
length muzzle that's rounded on
top. The Bullmastiff has a chiseled
head with visible cheekbones,
a broad, blunt muzzle, and
lips that are loose but not
pendulous.

Bullmastiff

TheDOGnosis

American Staffordshire
Terrier

Boxer

Great Dane

Bullmastiff

Norpin Terrier

This little dog has the long body of the Norfolk and Australian Terriers and the longer legs of the Welsh Terrier, with markings of the Miniature Pinscher (more commonly known as the Min Pin). Whatever the crosses, though, he displays all the typical terrier characteristics: lively, hardy, enthusiastic, and bold by nature. In spite of his small size, he is no lap dog. He'll love being outside, whatever the weather. He'll become active and yappy if he's not given enough to do. And he's prone to chasing small animals. He'll also make you laugh with his energy and antics.

Norfolk Terrier

Australian Terrier

HEAD
The wide skull is slightly rounded on top and shaped like a wedge with a blunt end, like the Norfolk's. It's also long, like the Australian Terrier's, with the muzzle equaling the length of the skull.

Miniature Pinscher

Norfolk Terrier

BODY
The Australian and Norfolk Terriers have the longer back, while the Welsh Terrier's neck slopes gracefully into the shoulders, plus he has a level topline and good length of leg.

Australian Terrier

Norfolk Terrier

Welsh Terrier

TheDOGnosis

Welsh Terrier

Australian Terrier

Miniature Pinscher

Norfolk Terrier

COAT
The Welsh Terrier has a hard, wiry coat that lies close to the body, with an undercoat. The Norfolk has a straight coat with a mane on the neck and shoulders. And the Min Pin is black with tan markings on the legs, chest, and face.

Norfolk Terrier

Welsh Terrier

Miniature Pinscher

TAIL
Both the Australian and Norfolk Terriers have tails that are short and thick, and are set high up on the rear. They hold their tails up or out.

Norfolk Terrier

EARS
Like the Min Pin's, the ears are large, V-shaped, and set high on the skull. But Min Pin ears stand up. The Norfolk's button ears are the same shape but drop all the way over. This dog is halfway between the two.

Australian Terrier

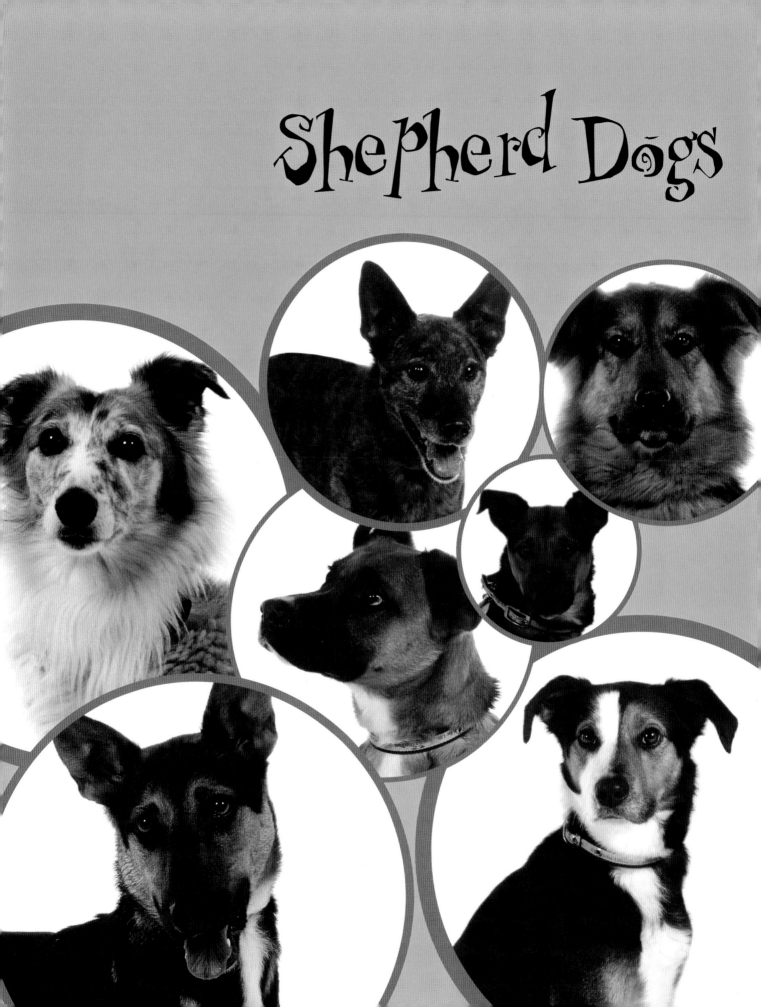

Shepherd Dogs

Malabeau

This is a large, powerfully built, alert companion. It seems likely that the major influences in his ancestry were herding dogs, probably both the Beauceron and the Australian Shepherd, along with a dog from the far north—perhaps a Malamute or a Finnish Lapphund. And is there just a hint of Irish Terrier in those ears? This is a reserved dog—typical of the shepherds and the northern breeds—who will be loving and protective with his family but stand-offish with strangers. He needs plenty of exercise and must also be adequately trained because of his potentially dominant nature. His instincts may otherwise overwhelm him, causing him to misbehave as a result, with potentially serious consequences. But he is eager to learn, and will form a very close bond with those in his immediate circle.

Malamute

BODY
Broad chest and powerful build like the Beauceron and the northern breeds.

Beauceron

Finnish Lapphund

EARS
Set high and folded over the top of the skull.

Irish Terrier

Australian Shepherd

COAT
Medium length like the Australian Shepherd's; thicker on the sides of the face says Lapphund, but the overall color is Beauceron black and tan.

Beauceron

Finnish Lapphund

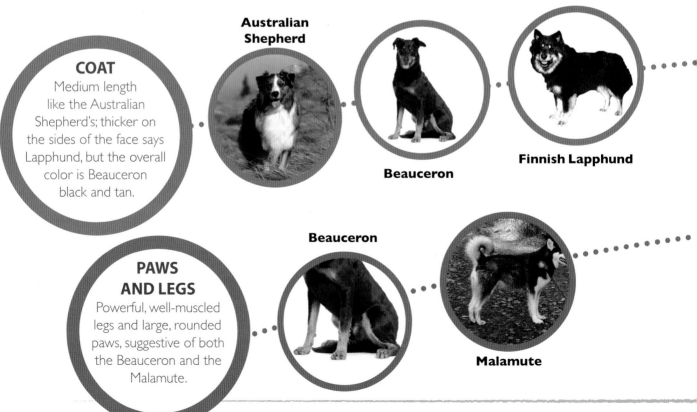

PAWS AND LEGS
Powerful, well-muscled legs and large, rounded paws, suggestive of both the Beauceron and the Malamute.

Beauceron

Malamute

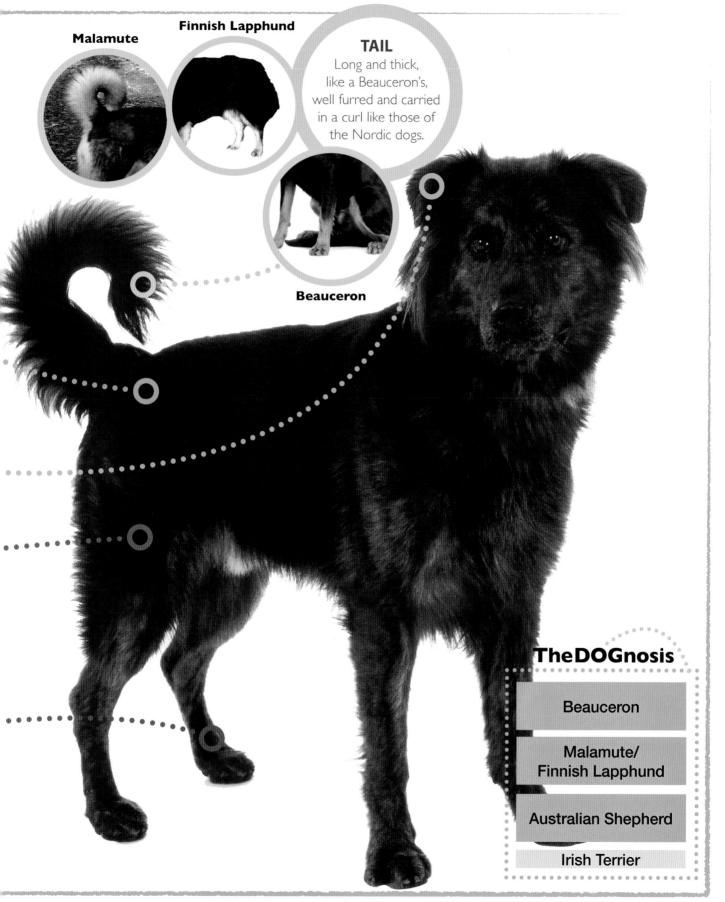

Malamute

Finnish Lapphund

TAIL
Long and thick,
like a Beauceron's,
well furred and carried
in a curl like those of
the Nordic dogs.

Beauceron

TheDOGnosis

Beauceron

Malamute/
Finnish Lapphund

Australian Shepherd

Irish Terrier

German Beagi

A quick look at this dog's head and you know at least one of his ancestors: the German Shepherd. It is quite unusual for one breed to be so dominant in a mutt's appearance. It's also interesting to see the head of such a tall dog on a body with such short legs. You might be thinking Basset Hound, but his legs are absolutely straight—which means it could be the Beagle's influence. There is even a white patch of fur on his chest, which supports this possibility. But that long, low body is not the Beagle type, either, so consider the Corgi. This dog is a lively character with plenty of energy, although he is likely not so responsive to training as a purebred German Shepherd might be (that hound independence from his Beagle blood).

COAT
Short, close-lying, and relatively coarse —that's Beagle—but the black saddle says German Shepherd.

German Shepherd

Beagle

BODY
Far longer than it is tall shows the Corgi influence, but the long, level back is German Shepherd.

Corgi

German Shepherd

TAIL
Long and held low, as a German Shepherd's, but bushy and a bit curved like the Corgi's.

Corgi

German Shepherd

PAWS AND LEGS
Forelimbs are short like the Corgi's but straight like the Beagle's, with strong paws.

Corgi

Beagle

The DOGnosis

German Shepherd

Corgi

Beagle

HEAD
Pure German Shepherd in every way.

German Shepherd

Golden Belgian Collie

This dog seems to have a little bit of everything. The Belgian herder, the Malinois, is crossed in with a long-haired (rough) Collie, and the Golden Retriever ancestry shows up in her coat. There may even be a little sighthound blood lurking in her genes, as shown by her relatively long, slender legs and elongated neck. Her weather-resistant coat needs little grooming to maintain its attractive appearance. She has a very intelligent, responsive nature, being descended from breeds that have been developed over centuries to work closely alongside people. This is an active dog; she has a tendency to become restless at home and needs plenty of exercise and room to run. Confined indoors and left on her own for long periods, she'll soon become bored and, eventually, destructive.

Malinois

HEAD
The muzzle narrows slightly. The light, lean wedge of the head suggests a Collie, and the Malinois has powerful jaws.

Collie

Whippet

BODY
The Malinois is slightly longer than he is tall, with a powerful chest, while the tucked-up tummy suggests Whippet.

Malinois

Collie

PAWS AND LEGS
Strong and straight parallel forelegs, like those of a Malinois. A Collie may have provided the muscular thighs and padded feet.

TAIL
The Collie's tail is relatively long and feathered, carried low when walking. The Golden's has a muscular base and may curl slightly upwards.

Collie

Golden Retriever

TheDOGnosis

Collie

Malinois

Golden Retriever

Whippet

Golden Retriever

EARS
One of each!
The dog's right ear
is triangular and drops,
like a Golden's. The left
one is semi-prick,
like a Collie's.

Collie

Golden Retriever

Malinois

COAT
Like a Golden's:
thick and wavy, with
a dense undercoat. The
Malinois is a rich fawn to
mahogany color, with
some white on the
chest.

Malinois

Rhodesian Bullspitz

Fawn coloration with black around the muzzle is a combination that is not especially common in purebred dogs, but in this dog's case it gives us a clear clue as to his origins, especially when combined with the shape of his ears. These characteristics suggest that he is part Bullmastiff, crossed with a smaller, lighter breed—maybe the Finnish Spitz or the Norwegian Buhund. Bullmastiffs are intelligent and very loyal dogs, bred as gamekeeper's companions in the 1800s. His narrower face, along with his coat texture and body type, suggest the influence of the Rhodesian Ridgeback, perhaps with a little Labrador Retriever tossed in. This dog is a smart, loyal companion, anxious to learn, and will readily alert you to the approach of strangers.

Labrador Retriever

Bullmastiff

EARS
V-shaped drop ears are set high and back on the head.

Norwegian Buhund

COAT
The short, sleek coat is a Bullmastiff's, but a lighter chest and the black around the muzzle says Buhund.

Bullmastiff

Labrador Retriever

TAIL
Thick and powerful like a Lab's, set low like a Bullmastiff's.

Bullmastiff

Rhodesian Ridgeback

Finnish Spitz

Norwegian Buhund

Labrador Retriever

TheDOGnosis

Bullmastiff

Rhodesian Ridgeback

Labrador Retriever

Finnish Spitz/
Norwegian Buhund

HEAD
Reasonably short but tapering muzzle and broad head, suggestive of the Ridgeback and the northern breeds.

Bullmastiff

BODY
His muscular body, with a broad back and a barrel chest, is characteristic of all of these breeds.

Rhodesian Ridgeback

Wegieman Boxhound

A very clear shepherd dog influence is apparent in the appearance of this dog's muzzle and ears. He looks a bit like a German Shepherd or a Norwegian Elkhound (which one figures into the mix depends on where you live), but has a relatively short coat and a lighter build. His overall makeup suggests one of the Belgian herding breeds, as well—possibly the Malinois. However, his brindle coloration is very distinctive and is not seen in the shepherd breeds. Among the breeds where you do see it is the Boxer, which his body type also resembles. The result lightened his frame and gave him a straighter back, without compromising his stamina. This dog has an athletic nature and plenty of energy, which means he needs a home with a big backyard, as well as plenty of opportunity to exercise farther afield.

EARS
Broad at the base, prick, and set a little wide—traits of both the German Shepherd and the Elkhound.

Norwegian Elkhound

Malinois

HEAD
Strong and slender, with a tapering muzzle that is about half the length of the head.

German Shepherd

German Shepherd

TAIL
Carried quite low, with longer hair than on the body.

Malinois

Malinois

COAT
Short and sleek like that of a Malinois, with a brindle pattern, as is sometimes found on Boxers.

Boxer

German Shepherd

Norwegian Elkhound

Boxer

BODY
Athletic, with a relatively straight back, suggesting both a Boxer and a Malinois.

Malinois

TheDOGnosis

German Shepherd

Norwegian Elkhound

Boxer

Malinois

Petibeard Bor-Collie

You may be wondering how such a scruffy looking dog ended up with the shepherds, but the fact is that there are some scruffy herding dogs. This girl looks most like a Bearded Collie, a breed developed to herd sheep in the border lands of England and Scotland. A key difference is that her coat is much shorter and scruffier, though. One of the rough-coated French scenthounds (dogs who follow prey by scent), such as the Petit Basset Griffon Vendeen (known fondly, and more simply, as the PBGV), may be in the mix here. She'll need a quick brushing almost every day to keep away the tangles. This is very much an active dog (some Border Collie blood will reinforce that) who needs lots of exercise and a job to do—even if it's just playing with the kids.

HEAD
The broad skull and square muzzle suggest both a Bearded Collie and a PBGV.

Petit Basset Griffon Vendeen

Bearded Collie

Petit Basset Griffon Vendeen

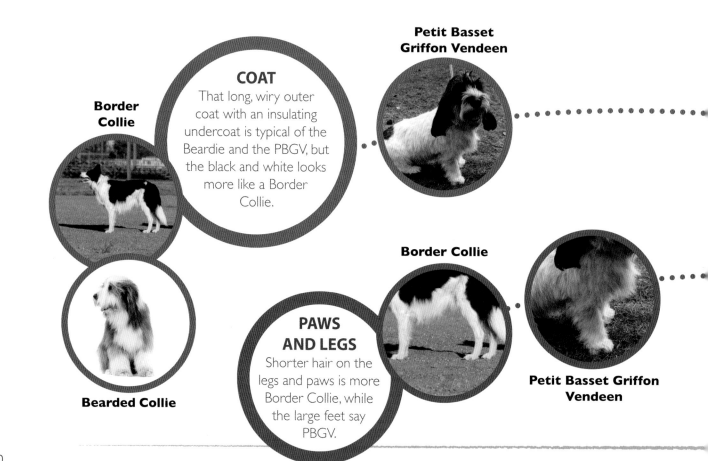

Border Collie

COAT
That long, wiry outer coat with an insulating undercoat is typical of the Beardie and the PBGV, but the black and white looks more like a Border Collie.

Border Collie

Bearded Collie

PAWS AND LEGS
Shorter hair on the legs and paws is more Border Collie, while the large feet say PBGV.

Petit Basset Griffon Vendeen

EARS

Set quite far back on the head and hanging down, like those of a PBGV or a Bearded Collie.

Petit Basset Griffon Vendeen

Bearded Collie

TheDOGnosis

Bearded Collie

Petit Basset Griffon Vendeen

Border Collie

BODY

Medium size, just a bit longer than the dog is tall, with a rounded rib cage—traits shared by the Border Collie and the PBGV.

Border Collie

Petit Basset Griffon Vendeen

Golden Butervita

Mutts can sometimes be very elegant, as this dog demonstrates. Her stunning golden-red, plush coat, beautiful head, and bright, round eyes are a very attractive combination. Her Nordic background is evident in her curled tail, reddish color, and the lovely shape of her head. Then add in a little herding dog, in the form of a Tervuren, and a coat texture like that of the Golden Retriever. The Golden shows up in her disposition, too. She is a responsive companion, easy to train and eager to please. This is a dog who just wants a job to do for you.

HEAD
Long, elegant head with a pointed muzzle and round, bright eyes.

Tervuren

Norwegian Buhund

TAIL
Well-furred and held low with a gentle curve, like a Golden's or a Tervuren's.

Golden Retriever

Tervuren

Golden Retriever

COAT
The relatively long, straight hair and golden color is Golden Retriever, but the deeper red comes from the Buhund. The heavier feathering on the neck, chest, and tail says Tervuren.

Tervuren

Norwegian Buhund

Golden Retriever

BODY
Long, broad, level back and a strong body overall, suggestive of both an Akita and a Golden.

Akita

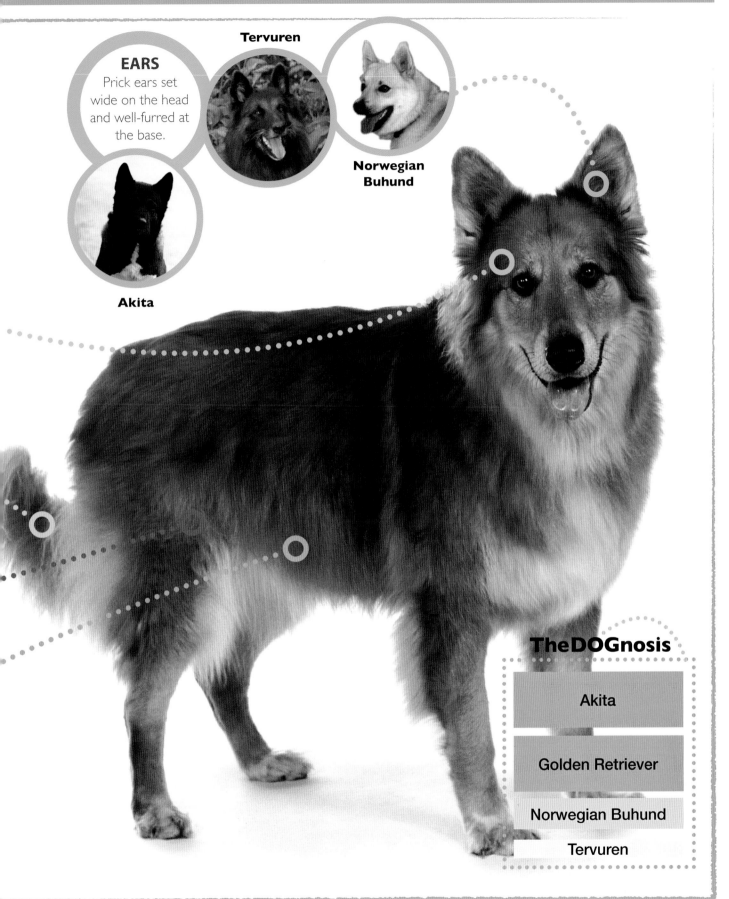

EARS
Prick ears set wide on the head and well-furred at the base.

Tervuren

Norwegian Buhund

Akita

TheDOGnosis

Akita

Golden Retriever

Norwegian Buhund

Tervuren

Boxshep Bullsla

This dog is determined and self-assured—a reflection of her likely ancestry of German Shepherd and Pit Bull. She is a loyal companion and will prove to be a fearless guardian, but she will need to be properly trained to prevent her from becoming aggressive with other dogs. Not that she's all serious-minded; she also has a very playful side to her nature, inherited from her Boxer blood. And her Vizsla side (the heritage of Hungarian hunting dogs) only adds to her trainability and her high activity level.

HEAD
The square skull, broad and flat on top, with strong jaws, is from a Staffie. The wedge shape with a tapering muzzle suggests German Shepherd, but those chiseled cheeks are Vizsla.

Pit Bull

EARS
Triangular ears are set high in the head like a Staffie's and fold forward like a Boxer's.

Pit Bull

COAT
Relatively short and glossy, with a reddish hue, like a Vizsla's, but longer, like a German Shepherd's.

German Shepherd

Vizsla

German Shepherd

PAWS AND LEGS
The hind legs extend out behind the body, like a German Shepherd's, while the broad and curved thighs are like a Boxer's.

Boxer

German Shepherd

Vizsla

Boxer

Pit Bull

BODY
Powerful, with a curve to the topline, a muscular physique, and a broad back: It all says German Shepherd and Pit Bull.

German Shepherd

TheDOGnosis

Boxer
German Shepherd
Pit Bull
Vizsla

Collinois Shepherd

Here is a dog who looks very much like a scaled-down German Shepherd, but his overall lightness suggests there may also be some Collie in him, too (specifically, the shorthaired, or smooth, Collie). The influence of both these herding breeds is also evident in the very positive way he responds to training. He is very energetic and playful by nature, and is ideal for a home with older children, particularly if there is a garden or backyard where they can run around together. He also needs to be taken out for walks in an area where he can be exercised safely off the leash.

HEAD
The German Shepherd's head is cleanly chiseled, and the skull slopes into a long muzzle that is somewhat blunt at the end. But this head is a bit narrower than a typical German Shepherd's —more like that of a Malinois.

German Shepherd

Malinois

COAT
The coloration—black saddle and facial markings, tan on the rest—is German Shepherd. But the splashes of white on the feet and chest are Collie colors. And the very intense black on the saddle is Doberman.

Doberman Pinscher

Collie

German Shepherd

German Shepherd

TAIL
On the both the German Shepherd and the Malinois, the tail is long, thick, well-feathered, hangs in a slight curve, and is carried low, except when the dog is excited.

Malinois

EARS

These are purely Collie ears: set wide on the head, triangular, and about three-quarters erect.

Collie

German Shepherd

Collie

BODY

The round and moderately long muscular neck, and the fact that the top of the shoulders is slightly higher than the rump, suggests a German Shepherd, as does the level back and gently rounded loin. But this dog's body is a bit lighter overall —more like a Doberman's or a Collie's.

Doberman Pinscher

TheDOGnosis

German Shepherd
Collie
Malinois
Doberman Pinscher

Swiss Border Collab

It's rare to see a dog whose facial markings are split right down the middle; it's a striking feature here. His coloration suggests one of the Swiss Mountain Dogs, most likely the Greater Swiss because that's the one with short hair. Speaking of short hair, both the Collie and the Border Collie can have long hair or short. This dog clearly takes after the shorthaired varieties. His mixed ancestry has resulted in a well-balanced, friendly mutt who thrives on attention and will adapt well to family life. Here is a dog who will happily spend hours playing with the kids.

Labrador Retriever

HEAD
The skull is wide between the ears, the cheeks are well-defined, and the flews (the lips) are tight but extend just below the jaw. Both the Lab and the Greater Swiss Mountain Dog have these traits.

Greater Swiss Mountain Dog

Border Collie

COAT
The texture of the coat suggests the Collies. Both have a double coat with a weather-resistant straight, flat outercoat and a dense undercoat. The coloration is Swissie: black, white, and tan, with black on the upper part of the body and the ears.

Greater Swiss Mountain Dog

Collie

TheDOGnosis

Greater Swiss Mountain Dog
Border Collie
Collie
Labrador Retriever

TAIL
The long, thick tail is carried down, except when the dog is excited, and is more thickly furred at the end.

Border Collie

Greater Swiss Mountain Dog

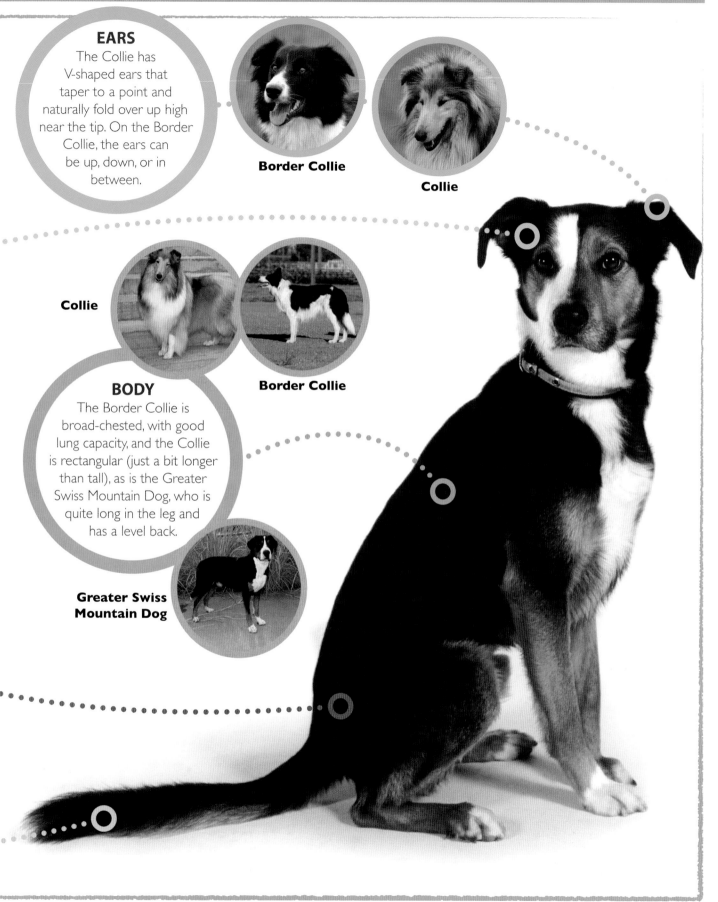

EARS
The Collie has V-shaped ears that taper to a point and naturally fold over up high near the tip. On the Border Collie, the ears can be up, down, or in between.

Border Collie

Collie

Collie

Border Collie

BODY
The Border Collie is broad-chested, with good lung capacity, and the Collie is rectangular (just a bit longer than tall), as is the Greater Swiss Mountain Dog, who is quite long in the leg and has a level back.

Greater Swiss Mountain Dog

Border Collita

Two types of Collies and the largest dog in Japan—the Akita—have contributed to this dog's ancestry. What else is in the mix is a difficult mystery to unravel. But the input of these breeds has resulted in a thick coat that will require a fair amount of grooming. He also has a wary nature, particularly when it comes to strangers, but is a loyal companion with those he knows well. Akitas have a tendency to be aggressive with other dogs, but the gentler Collie nature should help balance that trait.

EARS
The Border Collie can have ears that are up or ears that are down. If they are drop ears, they should not be too large or hang like a scenthound's ears.

BODY
Big, firmly muscled, with a wide, deep chest and level back, suggestive of an Akita. Like a Border Collie, he is athletic and a bit longer than tall, supported by powerful hips and thighs.

Border Collie

Akita

Akita

TAIL
The Akita has a large and full tail, set high and carried up and curled, with full, straight, coarse hair. The Collie has a well-furred tail with an upward swirl at the tip.

Collie

HEAD
This head has the refinement of a Collie's—a lean wedge that tapers cleanly to the tip of the well-rounded muzzle. But there's also something a bit broader and flatter about it, and that's the Border Collie influence.

Collie

Border Collie

TheDOGnosis

Collie
Akita
Border Collie

Border Collie

Collie

COAT
This is the Akita's double coat with a thick undercoat and a straight, harsh outercoat that stands off the body. But there's a little too much brown and black for an Akita—the coloration is more like a Collie's.

Akita

Tervman Rottamute

The influence of some of the larger working breeds can clearly be seen in this dog—her head suggests Rottweiler and the density of her coat means perhaps a Malamute (bred in Alaska), but there is definitely some shepherd in the mix as well. Her size means she will need a lot of space and plenty of off-leash exercise. She has an active nature, and wants to be trained and kept busy. She is also an alert guardian. Dogs of this type tend to be good with children, especially teenagers. They may be too powerful for younger children, although their large size enables them to withstand rough-and-tumble play.

Rottweiler

HEAD
The Rottweiler's head is of medium length, broad between the ears, and powerful, with a well-muscled neck. The Malamute's is moderately rounded between the ears with a large, bulky muzzle.

Malamute

COAT
The Tervuren's coat is long, straight, and dense, and the Malamute's is medium-long and very thick. The pattern is a German Shepherd's—tan with a black saddle and black markings on the head.

Malamute

Tervuren

Tervuren

German Shepherd

LEGS AND PAWS
Strong, straight, parallel legs are like the Rottweiler's and Tervuren's. The large, compact feet are from the Malamute.

Malamute

Rottweiler

EARS

These ears are a cross between the German Shepherd's large V-shaped prick ears, which are set on the sides of the head, and the Rottweiler's drop ears, which are also wide-set but hang down and forward.

Rottweiler

German Shepherd

German Shepherd

BODY

The broad, deep, roomy chest is like a Rottweiler's, while the straight back and the fact that the dog is longer than she is tall suggests a German Shepherd.

Rottweiler

TheDOGnosis

German Shepherd
Rottweiler
Malamute
Tervuren

Hound Types

Ibizan Whiphound

This dog is clearly of sighthound stock—bred to chase down game by following it visually rather than with his nose. His sleek body, head shape, and sloping back are all clues to his ancestry. He looks as if he is partly Whippet, although his very distinctive prick ears (sometimes called "candle flame") suggest that the Ibizan Hound or a similar breed has also played a part in his past. A friendly companion to those in their immediate circle, sighthounds have a healthy suspicion of strangers, and may seem aloof to those they do not know well. They also love to chase anything that moves. It is very easy to maintain his sleek appearance—a soft nylon brush is all you'll need. His exercise needs are quite modest, in spite of his athletic build, as he is suited to sprinting, rather than long-distance running. In cold or wet weather, however, he will need a coat.

Whippet

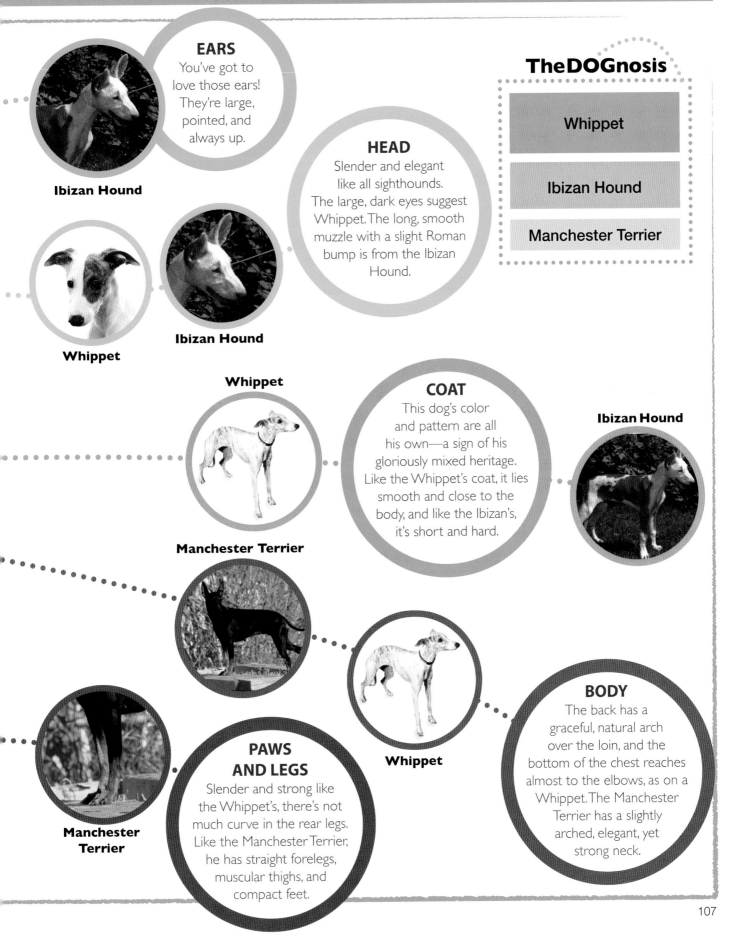

EARS
You've got to love those ears! They're large, pointed, and always up.

Ibizan Hound

HEAD
Slender and elegant like all sighthounds. The large, dark eyes suggest Whippet. The long, smooth muzzle with a slight Roman bump is from the Ibizan Hound.

TheDOGnosis

Whippet

Ibizan Hound

Manchester Terrier

Ibizan Hound

Whippet

Whippet

COAT
This dog's color and pattern are all his own—a sign of his gloriously mixed heritage. Like the Whippet's coat, it lies smooth and close to the body, and like the Ibizan's, it's short and hard.

Ibizan Hound

Manchester Terrier

Whippet

BODY
The back has a graceful, natural arch over the loin, and the bottom of the chest reaches almost to the elbows, as on a Whippet. The Manchester Terrier has a slightly arched, elegant, yet strong neck.

PAWS AND LEGS
Slender and strong like the Whippet's, there's not much curve in the rear legs. Like the Manchester Terrier, he has straight forelegs, muscular thighs, and compact feet.

Manchester Terrier

Grey Ibizan Slippet

This elegant girl is clearly of Greyhound descent, but her frame is slightly stockier than a purebred Greyhound and her head is not as narrow. Her typical sighthound profile represents one of the earliest forms of the domestic dog. Since humans started developing breeds, Greyhounds have figured into many dogs—added to various mixes to give each particular new breed speed and light-ness. This dog's coloring suggests that perhaps one of the Mediterranean hounds, such as the Ibizan Hound, may have played a part in her ancestry. And her head and ears suggest a little Whippet mixed with Saluki. All these sighthounds are active, independent, and love to run. Taking them off the leash in an unfenced area is always a risk, because if they see something moving out of the corner of their eye, they're off!

BODY
The long, level back suggests the Ibizan connection, while the deep chest and tucked-up tummy are from the Greyhound.

Ibizan Hound

Greyhound

TAIL
Long and held quite low, tapering, with a slight upward curve.

Greyhound

Whippet

Ibizan Hound

PAWS AND LEGS
Straight front legs and well-muscled hindquarters say Saluki. The strong wrists and ankles and tight feet are Whippet traits.

Saluki

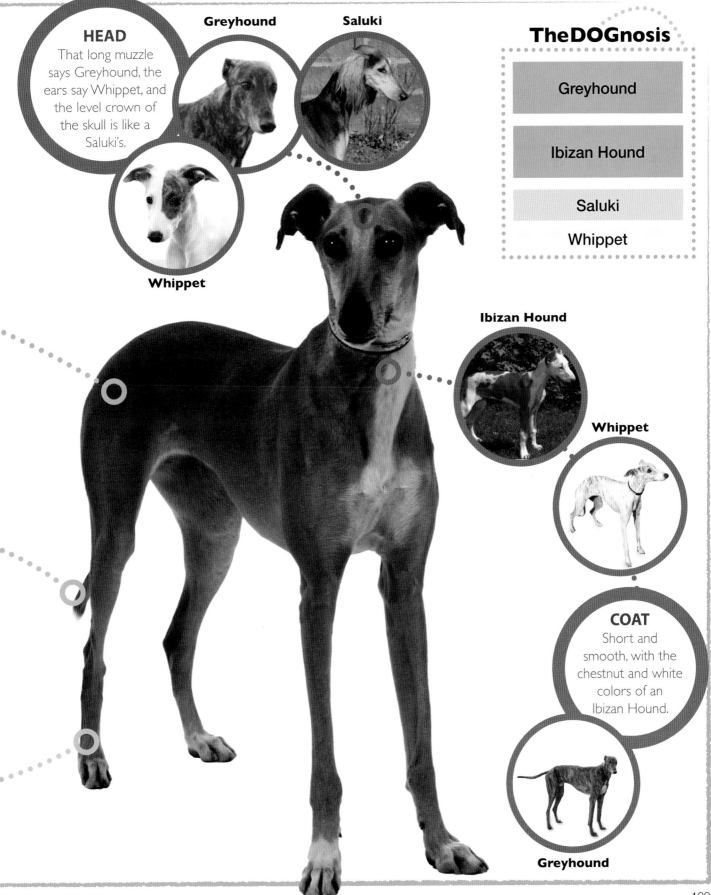

HEAD
That long muzzle says Greyhound, the ears say Whippet, and the level crown of the skull is like a Saluki's.

Greyhound

Saluki

Whippet

TheDOGnosis

Greyhound

Ibizan Hound

Saluki

Whippet

Ibizan Hound

Whippet

COAT
Short and smooth, with the chestnut and white colors of an Ibizan Hound.

Greyhound

Scodeeret Hound

The relatively coarse texture of this dog's coat is described as wirehaired. This characteristic is seen in many of the terriers and a few other breeds, and helps to protect them from injury when running through underbrush. This boy's tousled appearance is augmented by a beard of longer hair on the chin. He is also a large dog, and so could have Scottish Deerhound or Irish Wolfhound blood in his ancestry—or even both. Certainly, he is powerfully built and able to run. The shape of his tail and his relatively broad head also hint at a hunting dog ancestry, maybe one of the German Pointers. It seems quite possible that there may be a Labrador Retriever lurking in his past, too. He certainly has an enthusiastic nature and loves the outdoor life.

Scottish Deerhound

COAT
The wiry, harsh, tousled coat, along with the bluish-gray color, suggest the hairy hounds.

Irish Wolfhound

BODY
The broad, deep chest comes from the German Pointer, and the long, powerful stance is Deerhound.

Scottish Deerhound

PAWS AND LEGS
Broad forelegs with long front paws, and long, powerful legs front and back, say hound and more hound.

Scottish Deerhound

German Shorthaired Pointer

Irish Wolfhound

Labrador Retriever

HEAD
He has the strong jaws of a Lab, the square, bearded muzzle of a Scottish Deerhound, and the angular head of a German Shorthaired Pointer.

Scottish Deerhound

Labrador Retriever

TAIL
Well-covered with hair like the Deerhound's, thick and tapering like the Lab's.

German Shorthaired Pointer

Scottish Deerhound

TheDOGnosis

Scottish Deerhound
Labrador Retriever
Irish Wolfhound
German Shorthaired Pointer

Basset Corgi

It might be easiest to say this dog has the head of a Corgi, the body of a Basset Hound, and the eyes and tail of a Beagle. But of course, nothing is that easy in the world of mutts. How could three dogs mate to produce this little boy? Like every mutt, his mixture is something of a mystery, but we can see some clear characteristics that at least tell us he's part scenthound (dogs who track their prey by following a scent trail) with a little shepherd thrown in. This is borne out by his temperament; he's enthusiastic by nature (shepherd), but rather stubborn as well (scenthound). Training will not be easy, although perseverance will pay off. It's important to keep him well-exercised, so he does not become fat.

EARS
Large, triangular, tulip ears are rounded at the tips.

Corgi

COAT
The flat, lightly harsh coat is seen in Beagles, but the coloration is from a Corgi.

Corgi

Beagle

BODY
Deep-bodied and short-legged says Corgi, and that paunch around the middle shows a bit of the Basset.

Corgi

Basset Hound

Basset Hound

PAWS AND LEGS
Short legs with rounded paws are like a Corgi's, but the legs are not entirely straight and the paws are large and point outward, like a Basset Hound's.

Corgi

Beagle

Corgi

HEAD

Flat cheeks, with a strong, pointed muzzle suggest the Corgi, but the relatively long skull with large eyes is Beagle.

TheDOGnosis

Corgi

Basset Hound

Beagle

Border Clippet

This dog's head, coat, and color all say Border Collie. But she's taller and more slender than a typical Border Collie, and that's a clue that a sighthound, such as a Whippet, lurks somewhere in the mix. While Border Collies can have short hair, long hair, or something in between, this dog's coat suggests a little spaniel. Perhaps a Brittany—they're most commonly red and white, but they come in black and white, too. So what we have here is a mix of herding dog, hunting dog, and sighthound. She definitely likes to run. Taking off her leash anywhere outdoors is going to be an adventure.

Brittany

COAT
Wavy and medium length with feathering under the body, tail, and front legs suggests Brittany, but the overall look says Border Collie.

Border Collie

BODY
A relatively narrow body sloping over the hindquarters says Whippet, but from the front this dog looks more like a Border Collie or Brittany.

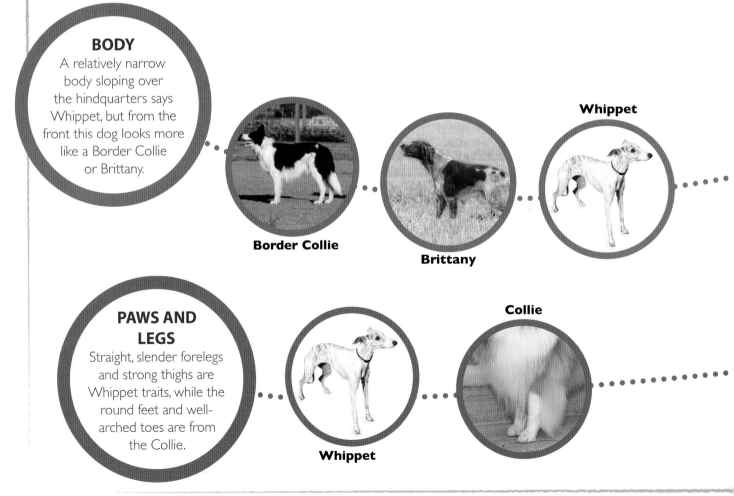

Border Collie

Brittany

Whippet

PAWS AND LEGS
Straight, slender forelegs and strong thighs are Whippet traits, while the round feet and well-arched toes are from the Collie.

Whippet

Collie

Border Collie

Whippet

EARS
Semi-prick ears are characteristic of both Collies, but they are spaced wide apart like a Whippet's.

Collie

Border Collie

HEAD
Slightly domed skull, with a medium-length, tapering muzzle and bright, intense eyes. One look at a Border Collie says it all.

TheDOGnosis

| Border Collie |
| Whippet |
| Collie |
| Brittany |

Irish Terhound

This dog seems to be a cross between a hound and a terrier. She's tall and slim, like a fast sighthound, but that wiry coat always makes us think of a terrier—until we remember that a few hounds also have that type of coat. The Irish Wolfhound comes to mind. And, oddly, because of those big ears, the Ibizan Hound does too. They are rare, but Ibizans do occasionally show up with a wire coat. Of course, the explanation may also be a lot simpler: A tall, red terrier, such as the Irish Terrier, could be in this dog's background. She will not do well in the city because she needs plenty of opportunities to explore and exercise. Her terrier-hound heritage may also make her wary of strangers.

Irish Wolfhound

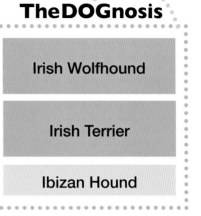

TheDOGnosis

Irish Wolfhound

Irish Terrier

Ibizan Hound

Irish Terrier

COAT
Dense and wiry, lying close to the body, not kinky or curly, and a rich red—all suggestive of an Irish Terrier. Red is also a possibility for the Wolfhound, whose coat is rough and hard, and especially wiry and long over the eyes and under the jaw.

Irish Terrier

BODY
The long back is characteristic of both Irish breeds. The tucked-up belly is a Wolfhound trait, and the slight curve of the topline looks Ibizan.

Irish Wolfhound

Ibizan Hound

Irish Wolfhound

TAIL
The tail is slightly curved and well-covered with hair like a Wolfhound's, but the curve and the fact that it is set low on the back says Ibizan Hound.

Ibizan Hound

EARS
Those large prick ears are all Ibizan Hound.

Ibizan Hound

Irish Wolfhound

HEAD
The long skull, with a long and moderately pointed muzzle, looks like a Wolfhound's, while the dark brown, intense eyes are like an Irish Terrier's.

Irish Terrier

Foxagle Rhodehound

Rhodesian Ridgeback

This dog is all hunting hound. Alert and powerfully built, he is a strong, almost effortless runner, thanks partly to his long legs. His scenthound heritage gives him good stamina, too—his ancestors followed quarry over large areas, hunting mostly by scent. He'll need plenty of exercise every day, and must be allowed to run off the leash. Although he has strong hunting instincts, thanks to his origins, he is otherwise a very gentle dog by nature and makes an excellent companion. He cannot be entirely trusted with very small dogs, cats, and similar small pets, though.

HEAD
The Foxhound's head is full but not heavy, with a clean neck and a straight, blunt muzzle. Like the Ridgeback, he has well-chiseled cheeks and his ears are set very high on his head.

Foxhound

COAT
The coat is short, dense, hard, and glossy like a Foxhound's. The Beagle coloring is evident in the tan and black with the splash of white on the chest and muzzle.

Beagle

Foxhound

Beagle

TAIL
Both the Foxhound and the Beagle have a tail set moderately high, which is carried up and has a slight brush at the end.

Foxhound

Rhodesian Ridgeback

Foxhound

BODY
A strong loin and back like the Foxhound, a deep and wide chest like the Greyhound, and a body slightly longer than it is tall, like the Ridgeback.

Greyhound

Foxhound

Greyhound

Rhodesian Ridgeback

PAWS AND LEGS
Long, straight legs with strong ankles are characteristic of both the Greyhound and the Foxhound, while the Ridgeback has compact, firm feet with thick pads and well-arched toes.

TheDOGnosis

Foxhound
Beagle
Rhodesian Ridgeback
Greyhound

Scottish Grey Zoiluki

This dog's long legs, powerful hindquarters, long whip tail, and tucked-up tummy tell you he's a sighthound. He also has a deep chest and a good lung capacity, which means he has enough oxygen to accelerate very quickly. This dog is a sprinter, and you will have to be careful with him when he is not on a leash. His size, coat, and head shape make it pretty clear that there is some Greyhound and Scottish Deerhound in his background. Perhaps there may also be some exotic blood from the very elegant Borzoi of Russia and Saluki of Persia.

Scottish Deerhound

HEAD
Broad at the ears, with a pointed muzzle that tapers to the nose suggests Deerhound. Like the Borzoi's, the muzzle is level on top and the nose is large and black.

Borzoi

Scottish Deerhound

Greyhound

Borzoi

BODY
This is the classic sighthound shape: Athletic with good lung capacity and a tucked-up tummy says Greyhound and Borzoi, strong hip bones set well apart says Saluki, but larger size and bone structure says Deerhound.

Saluki

Saluki

Scottish Deerhound

Saluki

COAT
The Deerhound's coat is harsh, wiry, long, thick, close-lying, and ragged. The Saluki contributes an overall softer, silkier texture and feathering on the legs, shoulders, and ears.

PAWS AND LEGS
The long, broad, straight forelegs, and powerful hindquarters are Deerhound traits. The Saluki contributes feet of moderate length that are not overly compact and are well-arched.

Saluki

Greyhound

Scottish Deerhound

EARS
Both the Greyhound and the Borzoi have small ears that are folded back when at rest but are pulled forward and become semi-prick when the dog is at attention. The Deerhound's ears are always darker than the general body color.

Borzoi

TheDOGnosis

Scottish Deerhound

Greyhound

Borzoi

Saluki

Scottish Deerhound

Foxy Whipspring

Smooth Fox Terrier

Whippet

Looking at this dog's coloration, long legs, and body profile, a scenthound, such as a Foxhound (or a Hamiltonstovare, if you live in Scandinavia), comes to mind. Yet his muzzle is longer and his ears are smaller and are set farther back on his head. A look at the Smooth Fox Terrier accounts for some of these differences. A bit of sighthound is evident in his elegant body, too. He's got plenty of stamina when he's exercising, and is going to be an active dog with a mind of his own. He will need training that takes into account the fact that he is easily distracted by interesting scents and moving objects.

COAT

The tricolor pattern is typical scenthound, as is the short, hard, dense, glossy coat. But the speckling on the legs suggests the English Springer Spaniel.

English Springer Spaniel

Hamiltonstovare

HEAD

The skull is long and flat on top, with not much of a break between the forehead and the muzzle, and strong jaws, like the Fox Terrier's. Wide between the ears and tapering to the nose is a Whippet trait.

EARS

The Fox Terrier has small, V-shaped, button ears that are set high on the head, like this dog, but the terrier's ears fall forward. These ears fall more to the side, like those of the scenthounds.

TheDOGnosis

Foxhound/ Hamiltonstovare

Smooth Fox Terrier

Whippet

English Springer Spaniel

Smooth Fox Terrier

Foxhound

Hamiltonstovare

Whippet

BODY

The absolutely level topline and relatively straight thighs indicate the scenthounds, but the slender build and tucked-up tummy are Whippet traits.

Foxhound

Whippet

Foxhound

Hamiltonstovare

PAWS AND LEGS

The Foxhound and the Hamiltonstovare have strong, perfectly straight front legs, especially at the ankles, and the feet are round and catlike. Like the Whippet's, this dog's legs are long in proportion to his body.

Great Grey Pointing Hound

BODY
Like the Great Dane, this dog has a long, powerful body, a level back, a wide chest, and a well-arched, strong neck. Like the Greyhound, he's tall and lithe but strong, with a tucked-up tummy.

Greyhound

A lively, athletic nature suggests this dog is descended from a combination of hound and working stock. He looks a bit like a Greyhound in build, but with a different head. Other large breeds are in his ancestry as well, probably including a Great Dane. The one-of-each ears illustrate how random genetics can be in mutts. It's also the case that the ears of young dogs sometimes fold over at first and later stand up. Training is important for this dog, just because he's so large. If he bounds up to people, full of exuberance, he could easily knock someone over.

Pointer

Great Dane

TAIL
The tail is thick at the base, tapering, and medium-long, like a Great Dane's. The Pointer's tail is also heavier at the root and is not carried between the legs.

Greyhound

PAWS AND LEGS
Long, slender, but strong legs like the Greyhound's, oval feet with tight, arched toes like the Pointer's, and the elbows set half the distance from the top of the shoulder to the ground, like the Great Dane's.

Great Dane

Pointer

COAT
This coat is short, thick, clean, and glossy. Greyhounds and Great Danes come in many colors and patterns, including brindle—even with the white splashes.

Greyhound

Pointer

HEAD
Like the Pointer's, the skull is as wide as the muzzle is long. The muzzle is deep and strong, and the flews (lips) don't hang loosely. Like the Greyhound's, the skull is long and wide between the ears. The eyes are round and are set wide apart.

Great Dane

Greyhound

Great Dane

TheDOGnosis

Greyhound

Great Dane

Pointer

Grey Zippet Hound

Who is this masked hound? She is certainly a sighthound—a dog who tracks prey by sight rather than scent. These dogs were once used to hunt both small and large animals, such as stags, wolves, and hares, and they needed to be fast and large. Sighthounds are sprinters, and they should, ideally, be exercised in an open area where they can run unimpeded, rather than in than in woodland, where they can never quite get up to speed. When she's off the leash, keep this dog away from roads and small dogs. Quiet and affectionate by nature, the big sighthounds make good family pets, although they are usually quite reserved with strangers.

Borzoi

HEAD
The Whippet's skull is long and lean, fairly wide between the ears, and tapers to a long, powerful muzzle. The large nose is a Borzoi trait.

Whippet

BODY
The Borzoi has a strong, level back, a deep chest, and a pronounced tuck-up in the tummy. The Greyhound has a long, strong, elegantly arched neck. Both are large, tall dogs.

Greyhound

Borzoi

The DOGnosis

Greyhound

Borzoi

Whippet

Ibizan Hound

Borzoi

Ibizan Hound

TAIL
The moderately long tail tapers to a point and is held down low near the legs, like the Ibizan Hound's. It is carried in a graceful curve, like the Borzoi's.

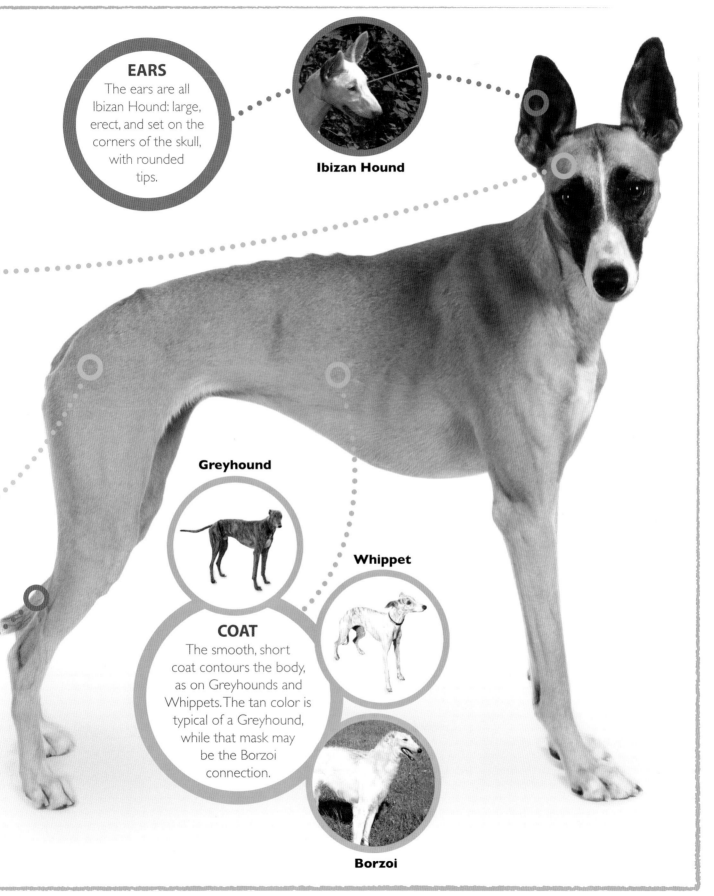

EARS
The ears are all Ibizan Hound: large, erect, and set on the corners of the skull, with rounded tips.

Ibizan Hound

Greyhound

Whippet

COAT
The smooth, short coat contours the body, as on Greyhounds and Whippets. The tan color is typical of a Greyhound, while that mask may be the Borzoi connection.

Borzoi

Greyscot WaterPoo

This dog is built for speed. There's a strong Greyhound influence evident in his physique, although he is slightly heavier than a true sighthound. There may be some Scottish Deerhound, as well—he's a large dog. His coat is very unusual, with that longer hair sticking up along his back, and that yields more clues to his origins. The grayish-white around his muzzle tells us that he's not a youngster. Older dogs can be great to adopt. They are house trained, and are often well-trained in general. And they're not as energetic as younger dogs, so even a large, athletic dog like this one can do well in an urban area.

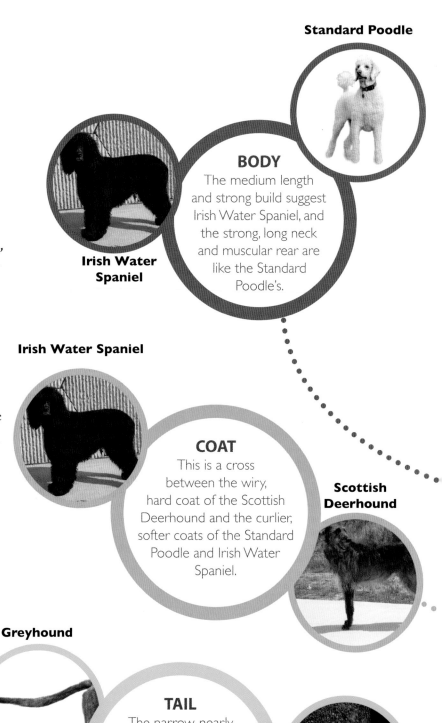

Standard Poodle

Irish Water Spaniel

BODY
The medium length and strong build suggest Irish Water Spaniel, and the strong, long neck and muscular rear are like the Standard Poodle's.

Irish Water Spaniel

COAT
This is a cross between the wiry, hard coat of the Scottish Deerhound and the curlier, softer coats of the Standard Poodle and Irish Water Spaniel.

Scottish Deerhound

Greyhound

TAIL
The narrow, nearly hairless tail tapers to a point, like the Greyhound's, but this dog's tail is shorter —more like an Irish Water Spaniel's.

Irish Water Spaniel

TheDOGnosis

- Greyhound
- Scottish Deerhound
- Standard Poodle
- Irish Water Spaniel

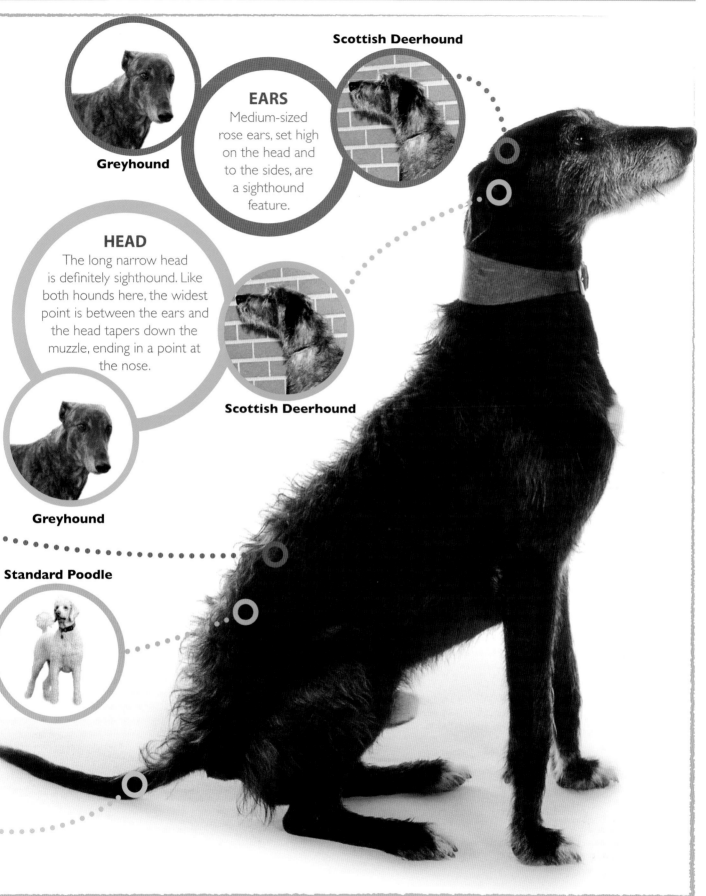

Scottish Deerhound

Greyhound

EARS
Medium-sized rose ears, set high on the head and to the sides, are a sighthound feature.

HEAD
The long narrow head is definitely sighthound. Like both hounds here, the widest point is between the ears and the head tapers down the muzzle, ending in a point at the nose.

Scottish Deerhound

Greyhound

Standard Poodle

129

Dobergrey Rottbeau

This dog looks a like a Doberman Pinscher crossed with a Rottweiler crossed with a Greyhound —and that's as good a guess as any. The Beauceron, a French herding and guard dog, has similar black and tan pattern, and is not as light as the Doberman nor as heavy as the Rottweiler. He may be in the mix, too. This is a strong, athletic dog. He will not run as fast as a Greyhound, but his overall large size means he can still get where he's going quickly. He may tend to be strong-willed, but training will help him be a great companion.

HEAD
The long head resembles a blunt wedge, like a Doberman's, and is broad between the ears, with almond-shaped eyes, like a Rottweiler's.

Doberman Pinscher

Rottweiler

BODY
The long, athletic body and slightly arched neck are like the Greyhound's, but that broad, muscular chest is all Rottweiler.

Rottweiler

Greyhound

Doberman Pinscher

COAT
The short, smooth coat has the characteristic black background with clearly defined rust markings on the muzzle, paws, face, and chest seen in all three breeds here.

Beauceron

Rottweiler

Greyhound

Doberman Pinscher

EARS
The Doberman's ears are positioned high on the head and are of medium size, but they're dropped. These flying ears are a Greyhound trait.

The DOGnosis

Doberman Pinscher

Greyhound

Beauceron

Rottweiler

PAWS AND LEGS
Long, straight front legs with smooth, long thighs and straight hocks (the area from the thigh to the ankle) resemble the Beauceron's. The feet are compact and not turned in or out, a Doberman trait.

Doberman Pinscher

Beauceron

Small Dogs

Manjack Chipin Terrier

This sleek, sturdy, elegant little dog is a tiny terrier. His coloration suggests both Miniature Pinscher and Manchester Terrier—the toy variety of the Manchester Terrier. And there's a bit more substance about him that suggests the short-legged variety of the Jack Russell Terrier. What he lacks in size, he definitely makes up for in character. He is very lively and quite noisy too, and is likely to be an alert watchdog. This is the sort of little dog who is always jumping up to be where the action is. Don't make the mistake of neglecting to train him just because he's small. If you do, he'll turn out to be quite a handful.

EARS
The Manchester's large ears are set high and back on the head, but the button ears are most likely from the toy variety of Manchester Terrier. The Jack Russell Terrier's ears are smaller and always drop down, but they fold all the way over.

Manchester Terrier

Chihuahua

BODY
Both the Manchester Terrier and the Chihuahua are a bit longer than they are tall. The Min Pin is compact, with a level topline and a well-developed chest.

Manchester Terrier

Miniature Pinscher

COAT
The Min Pin's coat is smooth, short, dense, tight, and glossy, and black and tan with a mask. But that white splash on the chest could be Chihuahua.

Chihuahua

Miniature Pinscher

PAWS AND LEGS
Compact, round feet with well-arched toes are typical of the Manchester Terrier, while the front paws that turn slightly outward are like the short-legged Jack Russell's.

Manchester Terrier

Jack Russell Terrier

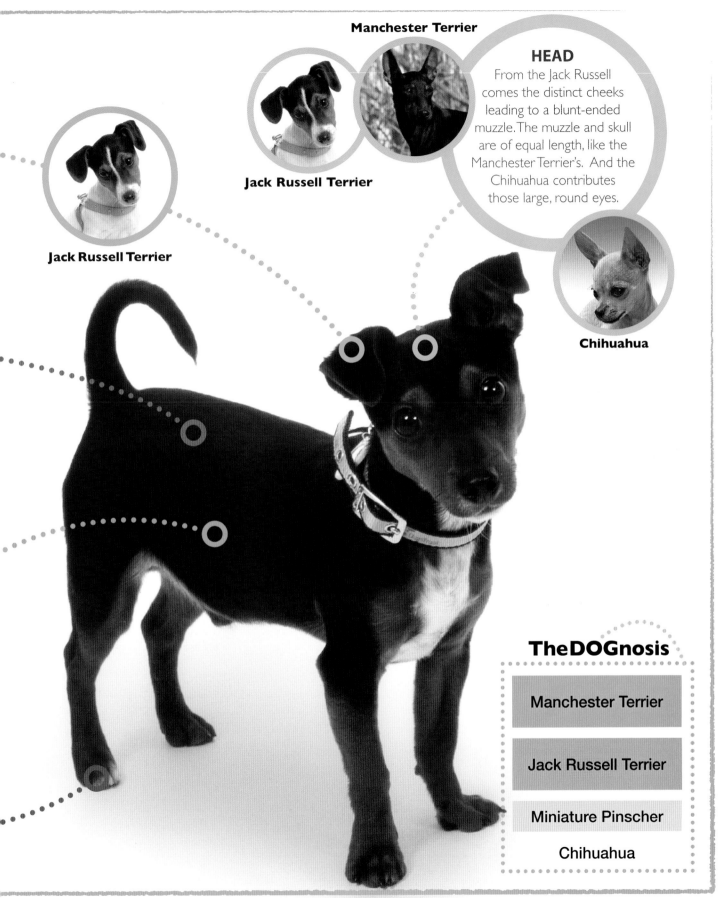

Manchester Terrier

Jack Russell Terrier

Jack Russell Terrier

HEAD
From the Jack Russell comes the distinct cheeks leading to a blunt-ended muzzle. The muzzle and skull are of equal length, like the Manchester Terrier's. And the Chihuahua contributes those large, round eyes.

Chihuahua

TheDOGnosis

Manchester Terrier
Jack Russell Terrier
Miniature Pinscher
Chihuahua

Manchester Ruggle Hund

There is definitely some terrier behind this very cute face: maybe the smooth-coated Manchester Terrier and the short-legged variety of the Jack Russell Terrier. But you can also see the Beagle in the black, tan, and white coloring, and that long back brings the Dachshund to mind. This dog is a very lively character who displays great stamina and thrives on attention. Like many terrier types, he is not especially accommodating in the company of other dogs. Although he's small, he's no lap dog. If he has the opportunity to kill rats or mice, his hunting instincts will take over.

Jack Russell Terrier

Beagle

Jack Russell Terrier

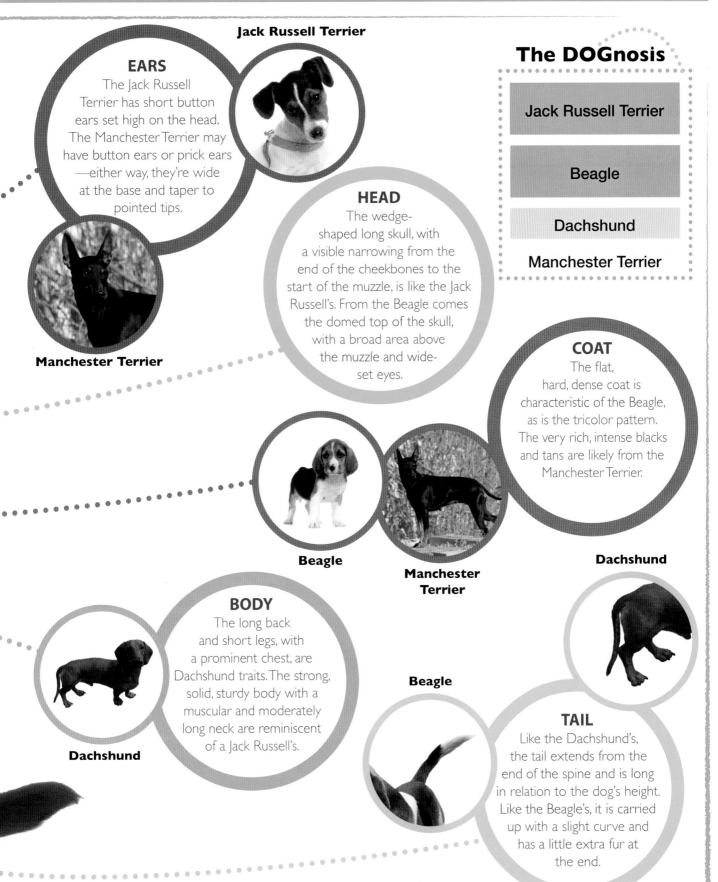

Jack Russell Terrier

EARS
The Jack Russell Terrier has short button ears set high on the head. The Manchester Terrier may have button ears or prick ears—either way, they're wide at the base and taper to pointed tips.

Manchester Terrier

HEAD
The wedge-shaped long skull, with a visible narrowing from the end of the cheekbones to the start of the muzzle, is like the Jack Russell's. From the Beagle comes the domed top of the skull, with a broad area above the muzzle and wide-set eyes.

The DOGnosis

Jack Russell Terrier
Beagle
Dachshund
Manchester Terrier

COAT
The flat, hard, dense coat is characteristic of the Beagle, as is the tricolor pattern. The very rich, intense blacks and tans are likely from the Manchester Terrier.

Beagle

Manchester Terrier

Dachshund

BODY
The long back and short legs, with a prominent chest, are Dachshund traits. The strong, solid, sturdy body with a muscular and moderately long neck are reminiscent of a Jack Russell's.

Dachshund

Beagle

TAIL
Like the Dachshund's, the tail extends from the end of the spine and is long in relation to the dog's height. Like the Beagle's, it is carried up with a slight curve and has a little extra fur at the end.

Aussietan Corgipin

This dog's most striking characteristic is his large ears, but equally important are the shape of his face and his well-furred tail. All three make us think of the Corgi—the Cardigan Welsh Corgi in particular. (There are two types of Corgis: Pembroke Welsh Corgi and Cardigan Welsh Corgi. In this case, the Cardigan is more likely because this dog has a tail, unlike the Pembroke, and a tricolor coat.) The relatively short legs and long body, plus the head shape, also suggest an Australian Cattle Dog. Both are bold dogs who are not easily intimidated. This is a reflection of the work they were bred for: snapping at the heels of reluctant cattle to encourage them to move.

HEAD
This is the general shape of a Corgi's head, with wide cheeks set into a strong, short neck, but the skull and muzzle of this dog are not as long as the Corgi's. For overall head size and muzzle length, the Australian Cattle Dog is a better match.

Australian Cattle Dog

Corgi

EARS
Those are Corgi ears, pure and simple: erect, with rounded tips—classic tulip ears.

Corgi

TAIL
The tail is set fairly low on the body line and reaches down below the thighs. It's well furred on the underside, like both the Corgi's and the Australian Cattle Dog's.

Australian Cattle Dog

Australian Cattle Dog

BODY
The short, strong body, moderately short neck, and good depth of ribs all suggest a Tibetan Spaniel. The body is longer than it is tall, but the legs are still fairly long, like the Australian Cattle Dog's.

Tibetan Spaniel

Corgi

Miniature Pinscher

Corgi

COAT
The medium-length, dense double coat, and straight and slightly harsh outer-coat is typical of an Australian Cattle Dog. But those markings are all Min Pin—except for the white splash on the chest. So we'll have to say Corgi here too.

Australian Cattle Dog

TheDOGnosis

Corgi
Australian Cattle Dog
Miniature Pinscher
Tibetan Spaniel

Tibetan Jackpuchi

Chihuahua

The smooth coat and broad skull on this dog point to her being part Chihuahua, which helps to explain her rather excitable nature and the way she may start shivering when she is excited or simply nervous. There is also some terrier in her past, with Jack Russell Terrier stock almost certainly being involved, as reflected in her color and pattern. But she's a solid little dog, and that suggests a thicker-set toy breed, such as a Pug, also played a role in her ancestry. There are also some similarities to a Tibetan Spaniel—a dog described as "assertive." In fact, this dog has a rather dominant nature, despite her small stature, as may become evident when she meets larger dogs. Early socialization and good training will help with that problem.

Pug

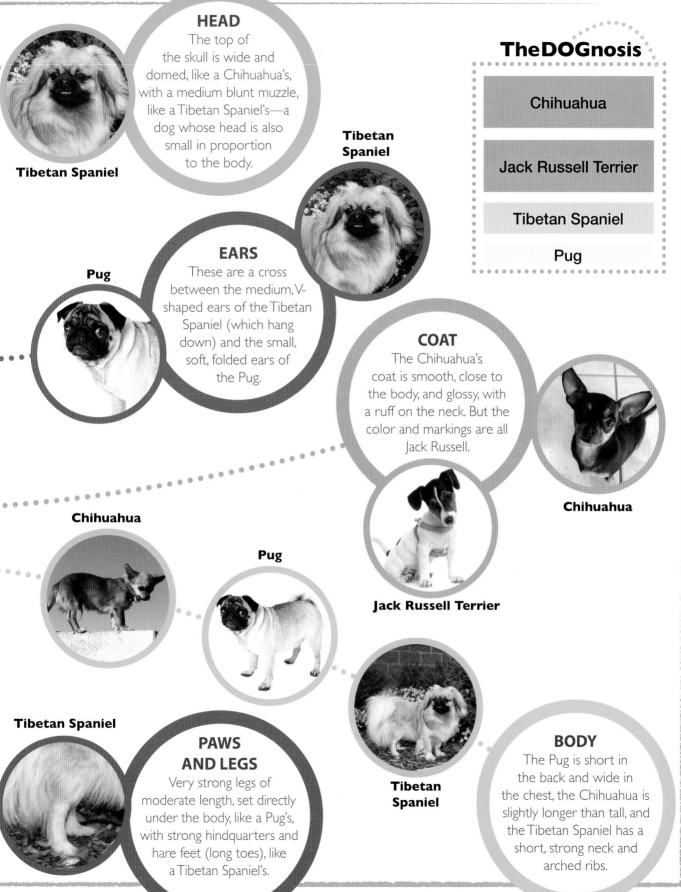

Tibetan Spaniel

HEAD
The top of the skull is wide and domed, like a Chihuahua's, with a medium blunt muzzle, like a Tibetan Spaniel's—a dog whose head is also small in proportion to the body.

Tibetan Spaniel

TheDOGnosis

Chihuahua

Jack Russell Terrier

Tibetan Spaniel

Pug

Pug

EARS
These are a cross between the medium, V-shaped ears of the Tibetan Spaniel (which hang down) and the small, soft, folded ears of the Pug.

COAT
The Chihuahua's coat is smooth, close to the body, and glossy, with a ruff on the neck. But the color and markings are all Jack Russell.

Chihuahua

Chihuahua

Pug

Jack Russell Terrier

Tibetan Spaniel

PAWS AND LEGS
Very strong legs of moderate length, set directly under the body, like a Pug's, with strong hindquarters and hare feet (long toes), like a Tibetan Spaniel's.

Tibetan Spaniel

BODY
The Pug is short in the back and wide in the chest, the Chihuahua is slightly longer than tall, and the Tibetan Spaniel has a short, strong neck and arched ribs.

Labrador Bachshund

This is a small dog with a big dog look—the not-quite-Labrador Retriever head and neck see to that. His short, stocky legs support a relatively long body, which, combined with the smooth coat and the way in which his front feet are slightly angled, suggest a Dachshund lurks somewhere in his past. The narrowing of the face is another clue—although there may be a bit of the Jack Russell Terrier in that, especially the ears. Jack Russells sometimes have short legs as well. And there might be a little scenthound in his background, contributing the white markings on his otherwise black coat. This is a very active dog, despite his small size.

EARS
Set well-back on the head and not large or heavy, like a Beagle's, but held out and folded, like a Jack Russell's.

Beagle

HEAD
Wide skull with powerful jaws, suggesting a Labrador Retriever, but a little bit domed with a tapering, slightly blunt muzzle that is not pointy, like a Jack Russell's.

Jack Russell Terrier

Labrador Retriever

BODY
Longer than tall, like a Dachshund, but the round shape, level back, and strong neck suggest a Lab.

Labrador Retriever

Dachshund

PAWS AND LEGS
Short legs with relatively large paws and no wrinkling on the skin. The slight inward curve on the front legs is especially suggestive of a Dachshund.

Dachshund

Jack Russell Terrier

Jack
Russell
Terrier

Beagle

TheDOGnosis

Labrador Retriever

Dachshund

Beagle

Jack Russell Terrier

COAT
Short, glossy, dense, and black, like the Labrador Retriever's, with just a hint of white on the chest that suggests Beagle.

Labrador
Retriever

Corgidach Brithund

This dog's rich chestnut and white coat suggests the likelihood of some hunting dog ancestry, possibly a Brittany. This is re-inforced by his friendly nature and the longer hair—called feathering—on his legs and tail, which is a feature seen in many hunting breeds, including spaniels. His short legs and long body suggest there could also be some Dachshund blood lurking in his ancestry—the longhaired variety may have contributed to his flat, wavy coat, as well. But his head is more a like a dog who has a similar body shape—the Corgi—with a cute pair of span-iel ears (the Brittany influence again). His spaniel and herding dog heritage (that's the Corgi) mean he is energetic. He'll thrive on long walks, where his broad nose will help him to detect a wide range of interesting scents. His short legs mean he'll be able to follow that scent under and into just about anything.

Brittany

EARS
Set high and folded down, like a Brittany's.

HEAD
Moderate size with a broad forehead suggests Corgi, but the tapering muzzle shows a hint of Dachshund.

Dachshund

Corgi

Dachshund

BODY
Short legs, long body, with a slight arch towards the rear —could be from the Dachshund or the Corgi.

Corgi

TAIL
Carried low, with longer hair, just like a Brittany's or a Corgi's.

Corgi

COAT
Medium-length, with some feathering, plus that lovely color with white patches.

Dachshund

Brittany

Brittany

TheDOGnosis

Corgi
Brittany
Dachshund

Pomhond

There is no doubt that this little dog is a member of the Spitz group, which is comprised of northern breeds. You can see it in his fox-like face, prick ears, and the well-plumed tail that curls over his back. In the 1600s it became fashionable to breed these big working dogs into miniature varieties, which became popular pets among the wealthy. Those with white fur, or brightly colored dogs like this one, were especially treasured as pets. This dog's coat is only medium length, but generally, selective breeding resulted in profuse coats on these little northerners. He is active by nature. Despite his small size and cute face, he could easily become yappy if he is not given enough physical and mental exercise.

Shiba Inu

HEAD
That cute, fox-like face is pure Pom plus a little Shiba.

Pomeranian

EARS
Prick ears, set high on the head and shaped like triangles, are like those of both the Shiba Inu and the Finnish Spitz.

Shiba Inu

Finnish Spitz

COAT
Medium-length, especially on the body, with a ruff around the neck—traits of both the Keeshond and the Pom.

Keeshond

PAWS AND LEGS
Less fur on the legs, with oval-shaped paws, says Keeshond, but the short stature is from the Pomeranian.

Pomeranian

Pomeranian

Keeshond

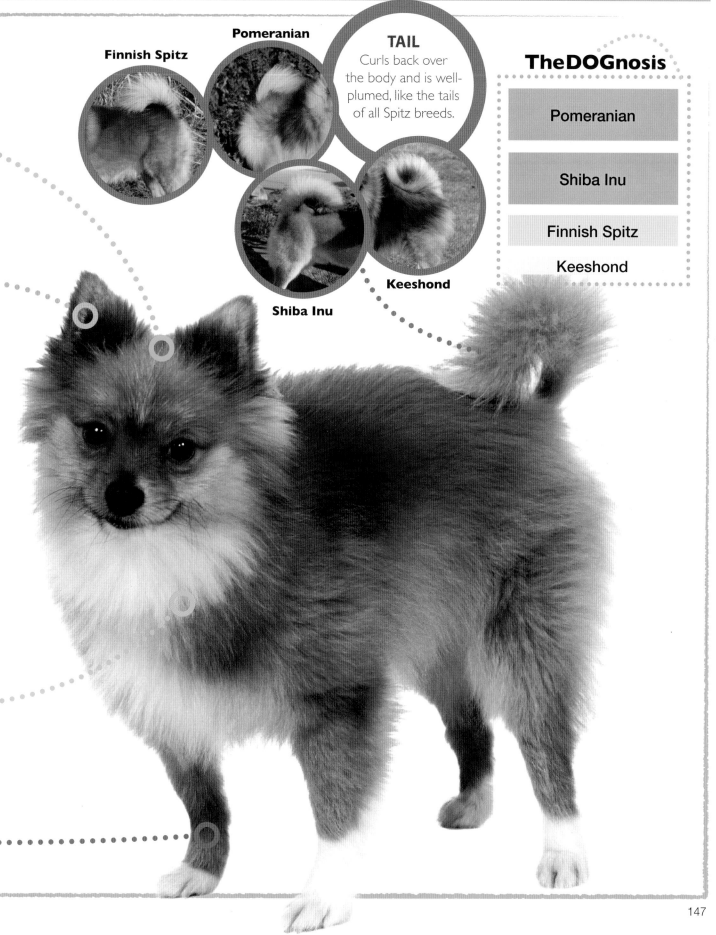

Finnish Spitz

Pomeranian

TAIL
Curls back over the body and is well-plumed, like the tails of all Spitz breeds.

Shiba Inu

Keeshond

TheDOGnosis

Pomeranian

Shiba Inu

Finnish Spitz

Keeshond

Pappy King Spaniel

Toy spaniels of various types have been kept as companions for centuries. This little boy is a descendant of these delightful pets, and has the friendly, affectionate nature you'd expect from a dog who has experienced centuries of aristocratic living and being the center of attention. His colors and markings say Papillon and Cavalier King Charles Spaniel. His ears are another give-away: The long hair is pure Papillon, but the fact that they droop says Cavalier King Charles. His head is large and his body is quite stocky—another hint of the Cavalier, with possibly a Jack Russell Terrier in the mix. Miniature spaniels are still hunting dogs at heart, so they're active and easy to train.

Cavalier King Charles Spaniel

Jack Russell Terrier

HEAD
Tapering, but not to a point, with strong, medium-length jaws.

COAT
Medium-length, wavy and profuse; likely inherited from the Cavalier or Papillon. The mostly white color and symmetrical head markings are also typical of those two breeds.

Cavalier King Charles Spaniel

Papillon

BODY
Broad-chested and square, giving the impression of strength.

Jack Russell Terrier

Cavalier King Charles Spaniel

PAWS AND LEGS
Short, sturdy, wide-set legs are typical of the Jack Russell Terrier, while the round feet are from the Cavalier.

Jack Russell Terrier

Cavalier King Charles Spaniel

EARS
Set quite high, with longer hair, says Papillon, but they drop like a true spaniel's.

Papillon

Cavalier King Charles Spaniel

TheDOGnosis

Papillon

Cavalier King Charles Spaniel

Jack Russell Terrier

ChiPomlapp

Short in stature but not in character, this is a toy dog with a very international heritage. You can see the Mexican Chihuahua influence in his head and the German Pomeranian and/or Swedish Lapphund in his overall look. (The likelihood of Lapphund depends on where he was born.) But then you've got that compact, square little body with the broad chest—highly indicative of a Pug (which originated in China). Put them all together and you've got both a lively little companion and probably a noisy watchdog, as well: a big dog in a little dog's body.

Pomeranian

HEAD
The Chihuahua has a very distinctive domed skull shape, and the pointed muzzle points us to the Pomeranian and Lapphund.

Swedish Lapphund

Pug

Chihuahua

COAT
Short and smooth but with some length in places, this coat is a happy medium between the longer-haired Pom and Lapphund and the shorter-haired Chihuahua and Pug. The black color suggests Lapphund or Pug.

Swedish Lapphund

Pomeranian

Swedish Lapphund

Pomeranian

BODY
Compact and square, with a broad chest, like a Pug's, but the level topline suggests Chihuahua.

Chihuahua

TAIL
Curls over the back, like those of the Pomeranian and the Lapphund—both northern breeds—and also like the Pug's.

Pug

Pug

Chihuahua

Pomeranian

Chihuahua

EARS

Ears are large and set low on the sides of the head like a Chihuahua's, but are pointed and erect like a Lapphund or Pomeranian's.

Swedish Lapphund

The DOGnosis

Pomeranian
Swedish Lapphund
Chihuahua
Pug

Bearded Australian YorkiePoo

This girl is the kind of mutt best known as "scruffy little dog." There are a few obvious influences in her make-up, some that are not so obvious, and others that will forever be a mystery. In some ways she is like a Bearded Collie, especially in terms of her overall proportions. There are some significant differences though, such as her shorter coat, that suggest another herding breed, perhaps an Australian Shepherd. And a Yorkshire Terrier can't be ruled out, based on the small, hairy, prick ears. There is something of the Poodle about her coat, too—when you remember that not all Poodle crosses end up with curly hair. About the only thing we know for sure is that this dog will need plenty of grooming!

Bearded Collie

Yorkshire Terrier

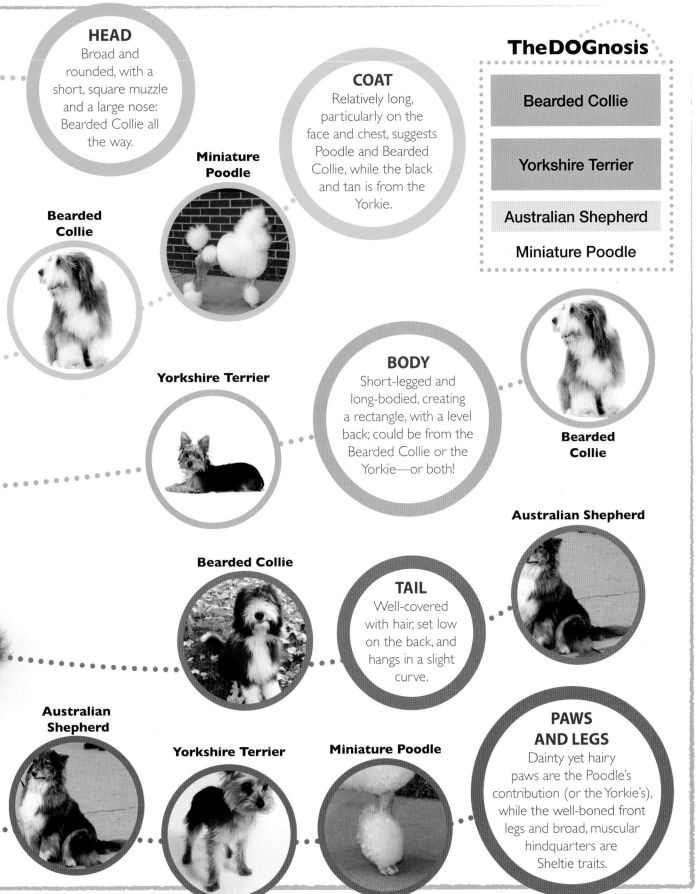

HEAD
Broad and rounded, with a short, square muzzle and a large nose: Bearded Collie all the way.

COAT
Relatively long, particularly on the face and chest, suggests Poodle and Bearded Collie, while the black and tan is from the Yorkie.

TheDOGnosis

Bearded Collie

Yorkshire Terrier

Australian Shepherd

Miniature Poodle

Miniature Poodle

Bearded Collie

Yorkshire Terrier

BODY
Short-legged and long-bodied, creating a rectangle, with a level back; could be from the Bearded Collie or the Yorkie—or both!

Bearded Collie

Australian Shepherd

Bearded Collie

TAIL
Well-covered with hair, set low on the back, and hangs in a slight curve.

Australian Shepherd

PAWS AND LEGS
Dainty yet hairy paws are the Poodle's contribution (or the Yorkie's), while the well-boned front legs and broad, muscular hindquarters are Sheltie traits.

Yorkshire Terrier

Miniature Poodle

153

Basspei Pughund

It is obvious this is not one of the giants of the dog world. Her short legs suggest that probably a Basset Hound played a significant role, but everything else is up for grabs—especially the ears! The black mask on her face is quite distinctive, possibly passed on from a Pug. But, depending on her precise origins, there may even be a hint of that other Chinese breed, the Shar-Pei, in her ancestry. If you're having a hard time imagining a Shar-Pei and a Basset Hound getting together, remember that most mutts are the result of dozens of crosses over many generations. This is an active little dog with a sweet nature and a lot of spirit.

Dachshund

Basset Hound

TAIL
Relatively thick and carried with a curve at the end, like a Basset Hound's, with a pointed tip like a Dachshund's.

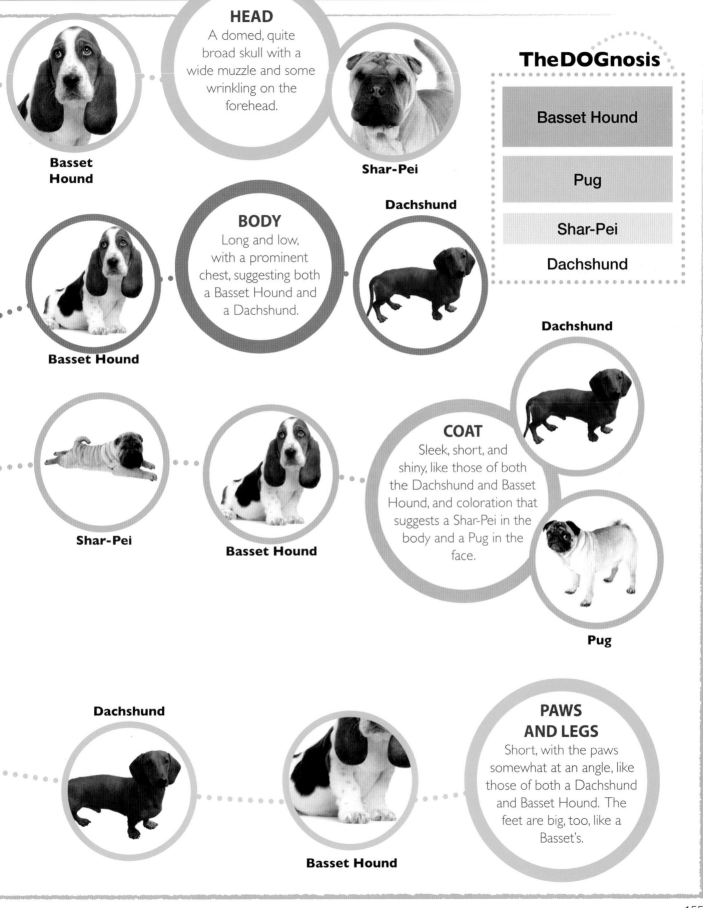

Basset Hound

HEAD
A domed, quite broad skull with a wide muzzle and some wrinkling on the forehead.

Shar-Pei

Dachshund

TheDOGnosis

| Basset Hound |
| Pug |
| Shar-Pei |
| Dachshund |

Basset Hound

BODY
Long and low, with a prominent chest, suggesting both a Basset Hound and a Dachshund.

Dachshund

Shar-Pei

Basset Hound

COAT
Sleek, short, and shiny, like those of both the Dachshund and Basset Hound, and coloration that suggests a Shar-Pei in the body and a Pug in the face.

Pug

Dachshund

Basset Hound

PAWS AND LEGS
Short, with the paws somewhat at an angle, like those of both a Dachshund and Basset Hound. The feet are big, too, like a Basset's.

Bullagle Mounterrier

It's really difficult to classify this dog. His overall look suggests a little bit of everything. He's slender in some parts and wide in others. He's small overall, but he has a big-dog look. He looks like a scenthound, a terrier, and a larger breed of working dog. With all this in the mix, he is an alert guardian, with strong protective instincts for those people who are in his immediate circle. He's inquisitive, and needs plenty of toys and exercise to keep him out of trouble. He can be quite noisy, too (that's the Beagle in him), and will bark to express his excitement or his concerns about strangers. He may also bark simply when he wants attention.

Beagle

French Bulldog

PAWS AND LEGS

The Beagle has straight legs with plenty of strength, and the French Bulldog's muscular legs are set wide apart with the feet facing slightly outward.

HEAD
The long, domed skull is very much like a Beagle's. But the tapering wedge shape, with a slight break between the forehead and the muzzle, suggests a Manchester Terrier.

Beagle

Manchester Terrier

The DOGnosis

Beagle
Greater Swiss Mountain Dog
Manchester Terrier

French Bulldog

Manchester Terrier

EARS
Somewhere between the large V-shaped erect ears of the Manchester Terrier and the triangular drop ears of the Greater Swiss Mountain Dog are these semi-drop ears. Dogs like the Swissie do raise and bring their ears forward when they're excited.

Greater Swiss Mountain Dog

Greater Swiss Mountain Dog

COAT
The overall coloration suggests Beagle and Greater Swiss Mountain Dog. The texture is also like both breeds: a hard, close, dense coat of medium length.

Beagle

French Bulldog

Beagle

BODY
This dog's back is short, muscular, and strong like a Beagle's, and he has a very broad, strong, flat chest like a French Bulldog.

Hunting Dogs

Chezsla Hound Retriever

This dog looks like a Labrador Retriever in an unusual color, but there's no doubt about his Lab ancestors. The color is a bit like the brown, or sedge, of a Chesapeake Bay Retriever, and a bit like the Vizsla's rusty red. The two retrievers in his make-up mean he loves to swim, and he'll also be a dependable, easily trained companion. The areas of white, the rounded skull, and the smaller feet suggest the contribution of a large scenthound, as well. Depending on where you live, it might be reflective of a Foxhound or a Hamiltonstovare, a Swedish scenthound.

Labrador Retriever

HEAD
The wide skull, powerful jaws, and blunt muzzle are from the Labrador Retriever and the rounded dome atop the skull says scenthound.

Hamiltonstovare

Foxhound

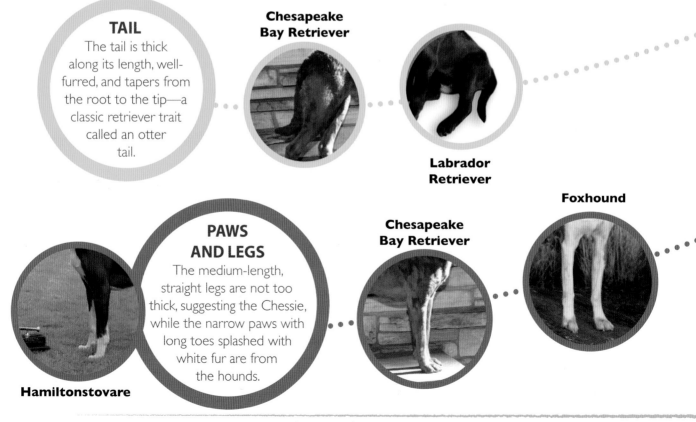

TAIL
The tail is thick along its length, well-furred, and tapers from the root to the tip—a classic retriever trait called an otter tail.

Chesapeake Bay Retriever

Labrador Retriever

PAWS AND LEGS
The medium-length, straight legs are not too thick, suggesting the Chessie, while the narrow paws with long toes splashed with white fur are from the hounds.

Chesapeake Bay Retriever

Foxhound

Hamiltonstovare

EARS
Large drop ears are set behind the eyes on the sides of the head, like a hound's, and hang down and frame the face, like a Lab's.

Labrador Retriever

Hamiltonstovare

Chesapeake Bay Retriever

Hamiltonstovare

Foxhound

Vizsla

COAT
The coat is short, water-resistant, and dense, like those of both retrievers, with Vizsla color and hound markings on the chest, face, and feet.

The DOGnosis

Labrador Retriever

Foxhound/ Hamiltonstovare

Chesapeake Bay Retriever

Vizsla

Vizslaraner

This is a strong, well-built dog with a variety of hunting breeds in his background plus, probably, a little bit of sighthound. It's the ears and the slighter profile of his body that suggest a hound ancestor. He is an exuberant, confident dog, and will make a great family companion. Crossing hunting dogs with hounds was once fairly common, to get a working companion who also had superior speed. In the old days, these dogs were not called mutts—they were just hunting dogs with all the right qualities.

Weimaraner

Whippet

PAWS AND LEGS

The front legs are long and straight and the muscular hind legs are relatively straight, like a Vizsla's. Those Whippet feet are compact, but the toes are a little longer than in our other breeds.

Vizsla

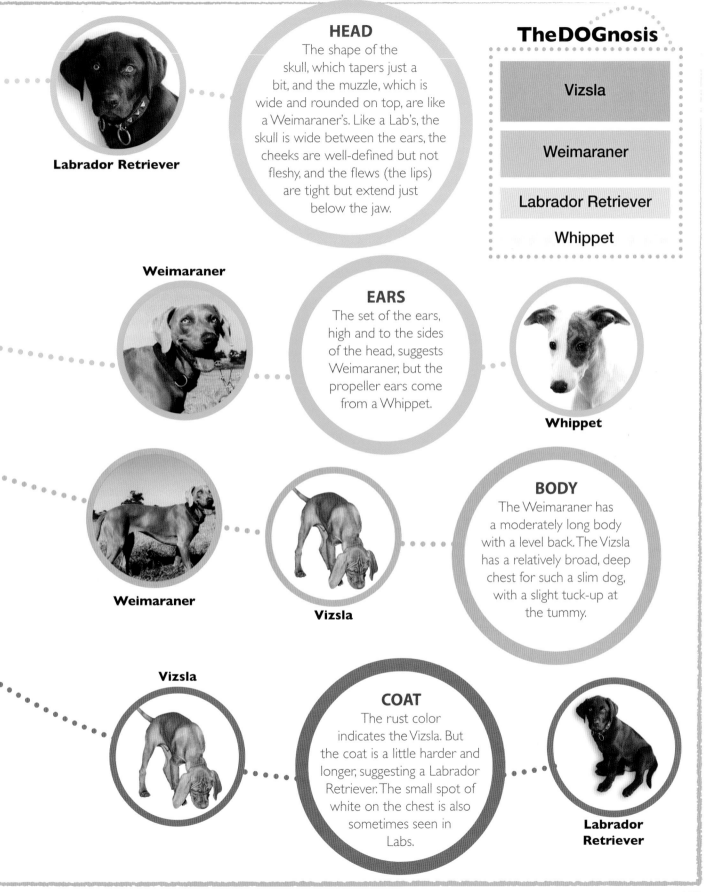

Labrador Retriever

HEAD
The shape of the skull, which tapers just a bit, and the muzzle, which is wide and rounded on top, are like a Weimaraner's. Like a Lab's, the skull is wide between the ears, the cheeks are well-defined but not fleshy, and the flews (the lips) are tight but extend just below the jaw.

TheDOGnosis

Vizsla

Weimaraner

Labrador Retriever

Whippet

Weimaraner

EARS
The set of the ears, high and to the sides of the head, suggests Weimaraner, but the propeller ears come from a Whippet.

Whippet

Weimaraner

Vizsla

BODY
The Weimaraner has a moderately long body with a level back. The Vizsla has a relatively broad, deep chest for such a slim dog, with a slight tuck-up at the tummy.

Vizsla

COAT
The rust color indicates the Vizsla. But the coat is a little harder and longer, suggesting a Labrador Retriever. The small spot of white on the chest is also sometimes seen in Labs.

Labrador Retriever

Pointy Dalhound

What an interesting and attractive mix this dog is! There's a German Shorthaired Pointer head, Dalmatian coloring with English Setter-style speckling, and the lithe body of a Greyhound. That smooth coat means grooming is very straightforward; stroking the coat with a special grooming glove or a soft nylon brush should maintain his immaculate appearance. However, those short hairs are stiff and tend to stick in upholstered furniture. This is an active dog and may not be well-suited to a life in a small urban flat. Regular daily walks and runs, rather than weekend marathons, are essential, to prevent him from becoming bored and destructive.

Dalmatian

PAWS AND LEGS
Small, close-knit feet with arched toes suggest German Shorthaired Pointer, while the straight, sturdy front legs with elbows close to the body, and very smooth yet strong thighs, are Dalmatian traits.

German Shorthaired Pointer

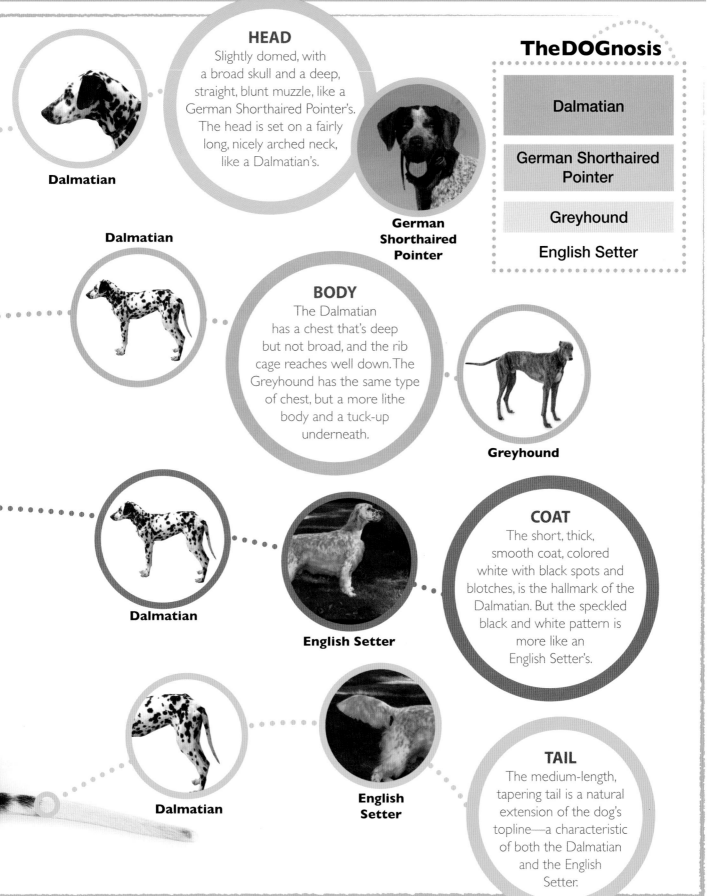

HEAD
Slightly domed, with a broad skull and a deep, straight, blunt muzzle, like a German Shorthaired Pointer's. The head is set on a fairly long, nicely arched neck, like a Dalmatian's.

Dalmatian

Dalmatian

German Shorthaired Pointer

TheDOGnosis

Dalmatian

German Shorthaired Pointer

Greyhound

English Setter

BODY
The Dalmatian has a chest that's deep but not broad, and the rib cage reaches well down. The Greyhound has the same type of chest, but a more lithe body and a tuck-up underneath.

Greyhound

COAT
The short, thick, smooth coat, colored white with black spots and blotches, is the hallmark of the Dalmatian. But the speckled black and white pattern is more like an English Setter's.

Dalmatian

English Setter

Dalmatian

English Setter

TAIL
The medium-length, tapering tail is a natural extension of the dog's topline—a characteristic of both the Dalmatian and the English Setter.

Retrieving Husky Hound

There is little doubt that this dog's ancestry includes some hunting dog genes. His color and build suggest both Golden and Labrador Retriever. But he is clearly lighter in body, suggesting a sighthound cross —possibly a Greyhound. His sleek coat and the position and shape of his ears are also like those of a sighthound. He is more active than a retriever, as well, and is able to sprint surprisingly fast. He'll have to be discouraged from chasing cats. The northern Husky heritage is evident in his tail and his white underside. All in all, this is a good family pet, with a gentle, supportive nature.

Labrador Retriever

Siberian Husky

HEAD
The wide skull with a broad nose is a Labrador Retriever's, but the tapering shape from the forehead to the muzzle suggests Husky.

Labrador Retriever

TAIL
Thick and sturdy like a Labrador Retriever's, but heavily furred underneath and carried in a gentle curl, like a Husky's.

Siberian Husky

BODY
This dog is longer than he is tall, with a stocky profile and deep chest suggestive of both retrievers, but his overall lightness is from the Greyhound.

Golden Retriever

Greyhound

Labrador Retriever

COAT
Relatively short and sleek like a Greyhound's, the color and density of a yellow Lab's, and the white underside and mask of a Husky.

Greyhound

EARS
These are called propeller ears, and they are sometimes found on some sighthounds, including the Greyhound.

Greyhound

Labrador Retriever

Siberian Husky

The DOGnosis

Labrador Retriever

Siberian Husky

Golden Retriever

Greyhound

Loxer Bull Retriever

The brindle pattern on this dog's coat, with black lines running like waves through a rich chestnut-red background, is especially striking. He is a stocky dog, even though he is not yet fully grown, and will be a big adult. He is clearly is from working dog stock, and therefore has quite a strong, determined temperament. He also has a bit of an independent streak, but, like all dogs bred to do a job, he responds well to training. He's going to need plenty of exercise, and probably loves a good swim—evidence of a retrieving instinct.

Boxer

HEAD
The broad, square skull suggests Boxer, and the long but blocky muzzle is like the Labrador Retriever's.

Labrador Retriever

TheDOGnosis

Boxer

Labrador Retriever

Bullmastiff

Bullmastiff

EARS
V-shaped ears, set high on the head and dropped over, suggest Bullmastiff, but the length and the rounded tips are more like a Lab's ears.

Labrador Retriever

COAT
The smooth, short coat with the brindle pattern could be Boxer or Bullmastiff, and the glossy sheen and dense texture are Labrador heritage.

Labrador Retriever

Boxer

Bullmastiff

BODY
Stocky and muscular overall. The long back is like a Boxer's, while the dip behind the top of the shoulders suggests Bullmastiff.

Boxer

Bullmastiff

PAWS AND LEGS
Very strong front legs with pronounced wrists and long, powerful thighs come from the Bullmastiff. The large, round paws are like a Lab's.

Bullmastiff

Labrador Retriever

Labra-Coat Foxtriever

The glossy coat and the head of this dog clearly reveal that a Labrador Retriever played a role in his ancestry. Nevertheless, he is more lightly built than a purebred Labrador Retriever. There are likely some other hunting dogs in his background, and possibly even a scenthound, such as the Foxhound. Friendly and lively by nature, this dog is an ideal companion in a home with older children, where he will have as much energy as they do. His keen retrieving instincts mean that he is always ready to play—especially fetch. He may not be well-suited to urban life, though, because he needs a lot of exercise. He is also something of a glutton, and requires plenty of opportunity to burn off the calories so he doesn't become overweight.

Weimaraner

HEAD
Broad head with a flat top, with nicely chiseled cheekbones and a blocky muzzle.

Labrador Retriever

BODY
Strong and well-proportioned, with a powerful chest, like a Lab, but not as wide and chunky as a typical Lab.

Labrador Retriever

Foxhound

COAT
The short, glossy parts are the Lab's heritage, while the longer parts and the hard texture, plus the color, say Flat-Coat.

Labrador Retriever

Flat-Coated Retriever

PAWS AND LEGS
Strong, thick legs from the Lab, straight front legs with well-arched toes from the Foxhound.

Labrador Retriever

Foxhound

The DOGnosis

Labrador Retriever
Flat-Coated Retriever
Foxhound
Weimaraner

Labrador Retriever

EARS
Large, set on the top and sides of the head, and hanging down, like those of both retrievers.

Flat-Coated Retriever

Pointing Greydane

The striking speckled pattern and body shape on this girl suggests some Pointer ancestry. Pointers find game with their nose, and that long, broad muzzle is just the right tool. But her head has a gentler slope from forehead to muzzle and those ears—well, you'd never find them on a Pointer! There seems to be a little bit of the hound in this dog, too; you can see it in the tucked-up tummy and the tail held down between her hind legs. Sighthounds hunt by following game visually. A dog like this, with two kinds of hunters in her heritage, is likely to be serious and hardworking. She is also big and energetic, and will need plenty of exercise. Give her a job to do and you'll find she's smart and easy to train. But if she gets bored, she could become destructive.

HEAD
Long, broad muzzle with loose lips suggests Pointer or Great Dane. The gently sloping forehead is all Dane.

Pointer

Great Dane

Greyhound

Pointer

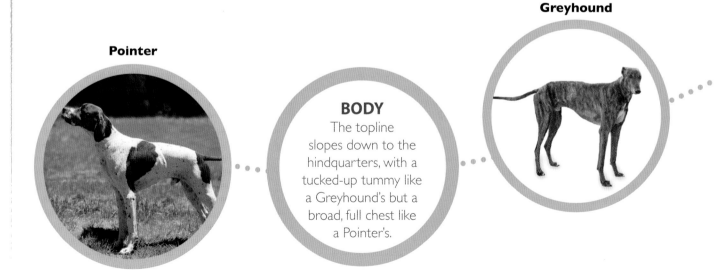

BODY
The topline slopes down to the hindquarters, with a tucked-up tummy like a Greyhound's but a broad, full chest like a Pointer's.

Great Dane

EARS
Set high and raised, like a Greyhound's, but hanging forward like a Great Dane's.

Greyhound

TheDOGnosis

Pointer

Greyhound

Great Dane

Pointer

COAT
Short and sleek, with a speckled pattern often seen on Pointers.

Greyhound

TAIL
Quite long and carried low like a Great Dane's, but tucked between the legs, like a Greyhound's.

Great Dane

Danish SetPoint

This dog seems to be part Pointer, although his head is broader and his ears are very different. He is a tall dog, and his black and white coloring helps provide another clue about his ancestry: He probably also has a Great Dane ancestor with the black and white pattern known as harlequin. His coat, with just a little something extra around the neck, suggests a hint of English Setter as well. Despite his large size, this dog is a very amenable individual, and his sleek coat means that little time has to be spent on grooming. Even so, his large appetite means feeding him can be an expensive proposition.

Pointer

HEAD
Broad and cleanly chiseled, with a long, rectangular muzzle—the Pointer and Great Dane are likely responsible.

Great Dane

Pointer

COAT
Short and quite sleek says Pointer, but the pattern looks inherited from a harlequin Great Dane and that little bit of fluff is most likely from the Setter.

Great Dane

English Setter

English Setter

PAWS AND LEGS
Long, straight forelegs say Pointer, while the tight, strong feet and speckled legs are from the English Setter.

Pointer

TheDOGnosis

Pointer
Great Dane
English Setter

EARS
Relatively large, set towards the back of the skull, high set, and folded over—it all says Great Dane.

Great Dane

BODY
This dog is as long as he is tall, like the Pointer and the Great Dane.

Pointer

Great Dane

Goldepeake Shepherd

One look at that body and you know there's a Golden Retriever somewhere in this dog's lineage. But her head tells another story. She lacks the square muzzle and the drop ears that are typical of retrievers. No, that head says herding dog. Maybe a Collie with those ears? Maybe a German Shepherd with that muzzle? And although we are used to seeing German Shepherds in black and brown, they do come in other colors. Whatever the specifics, retriever and shepherd is a winning combination: smart, easily trained, social, and good with kids.

EARS
Triangular and high on the head, like a German Shepherd's, but dropping at the tips, like a Collie's.

German Shepherd

Collie

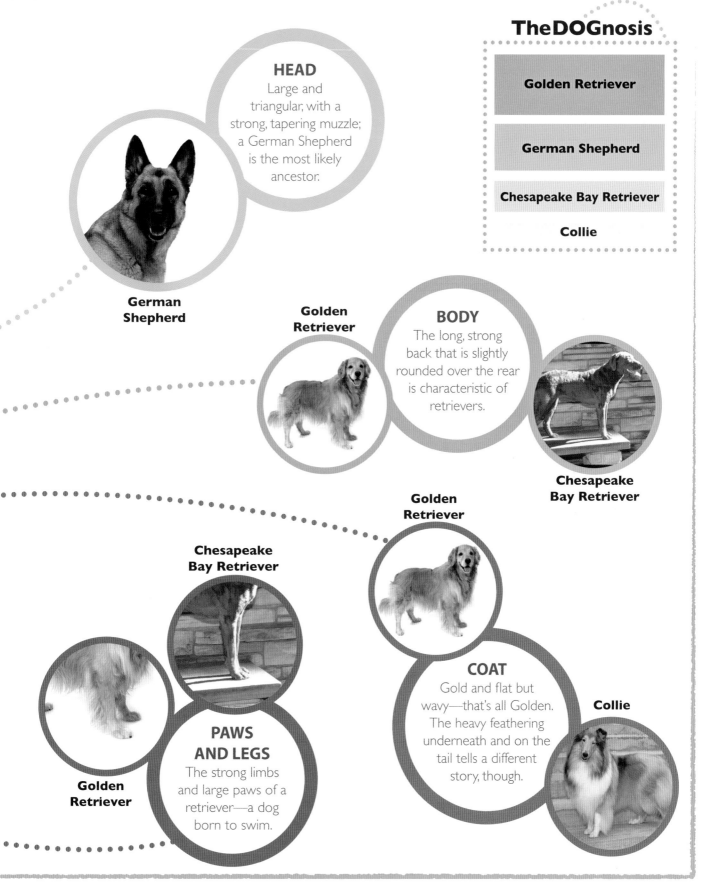

TheDOGnosis

Golden Retriever

German Shepherd

Chesapeake Bay Retriever

Collie

HEAD
Large and triangular, with a strong, tapering muzzle; a German Shepherd is the most likely ancestor.

German Shepherd

Golden Retriever

BODY
The long, strong back that is slightly rounded over the rear is characteristic of retrievers.

Chesapeake Bay Retriever

Golden Retriever

Chesapeake Bay Retriever

PAWS AND LEGS
The strong limbs and large paws of a retriever—a dog born to swim.

Golden Retriever

COAT
Gold and flat but wavy—that's all Golden. The heavy feathering underneath and on the tail tells a different story, though.

Collie

Designer Dogs

Labradoodle

Figuring out which breeds are in a mutt's background is always something of a guess. But these so-called designer dogs are the result of two lines of purebred dogs being mated, with the aim of establishing new types of dogs with predictable characteristics. The Labradoodle is a very popular example. He was first bred in the 1980s in Australia when a woman who needed a guide dog asked for one who would not irritate her husband's allergy to dogs. Still, this is not a hypoallergenic dog—Poodles just shed less. And he's just as active and smart as both "founder" breeds.

HEAD
The wide skull, with plenty of space between the ears, and a wide nose, is from the Lab. The moderately rounded top and the long, straight, strong muzzle are Poodle characteristics.

Labrador Retriever

Standard Poodle

COAT
This dog has a fleece coat, which hangs in loose, loopy spirals. It's a combination of the harsh, curly, dense coat of the Poodle and the flat, hard, short coat of the Lab.

Labrador Retriever

BODY
The Lab has a powerful build with a level topline. The Poodle has a deep and moderately wide chest and a rear that is broad, short, and muscular.

Labrador Retriever

Standard Poodle

TAIL
The tail is quite thick at the base and tapers, like a Lab's. It's set high up on the back, carried high, and well furred, like a Poodle's.

Labrador Retriever

Standard Poodle

Standard Poodle

PAWS AND LEGS
The Lab has very strong, thick legs with large, compact feet and thick foot pads. The Poodle has long, straight legs, front and back.

Standard Poodle

EARS
These are mostly Poodle ears—long and furry, set low, and hanging close to the head. But Lab ears are also set low and hang close, and the shorter hair keeps these ears manageable.

Standard Poodle

Labrador Retriever

Standard Poodle

TheDOGnosis

Labrador Retriever

Standard Poodle

Labrador Retriever

Puggle

Puggles are the progeny of Pugs and Beagles, and they seem to have gotten the best of both. Everything that is extreme in the Pug and the Beagle is offered in moderation in the Puggle. This is an energetic little hound with the playfulness of a companion dog. They are social and affectionate, and are a bit easier to train than the typical Beagle. They will enjoy their exercise, but will also accept a good cuddle. And they get along well with children, other dogs, and most other pets. However, they do retain that Beagle tendency to bark and howl.

TAIL

The tail is a bit thick and set quite high on the back, like both breeds. The gentle curl is the middle ground between the Beagle's straight tail and the Pug's tight double curl.

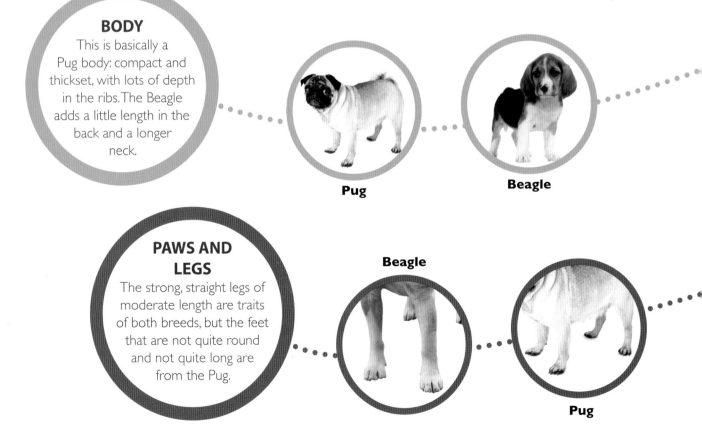

Beagle

Pug

BODY

This is basically a Pug body: compact and thickset, with lots of depth in the ribs. The Beagle adds a little length in the back and a longer neck.

Pug

Beagle

PAWS AND LEGS

The strong, straight legs of moderate length are traits of both breeds, but the feet that are not quite round and not quite long are from the Pug.

Beagle

Pug

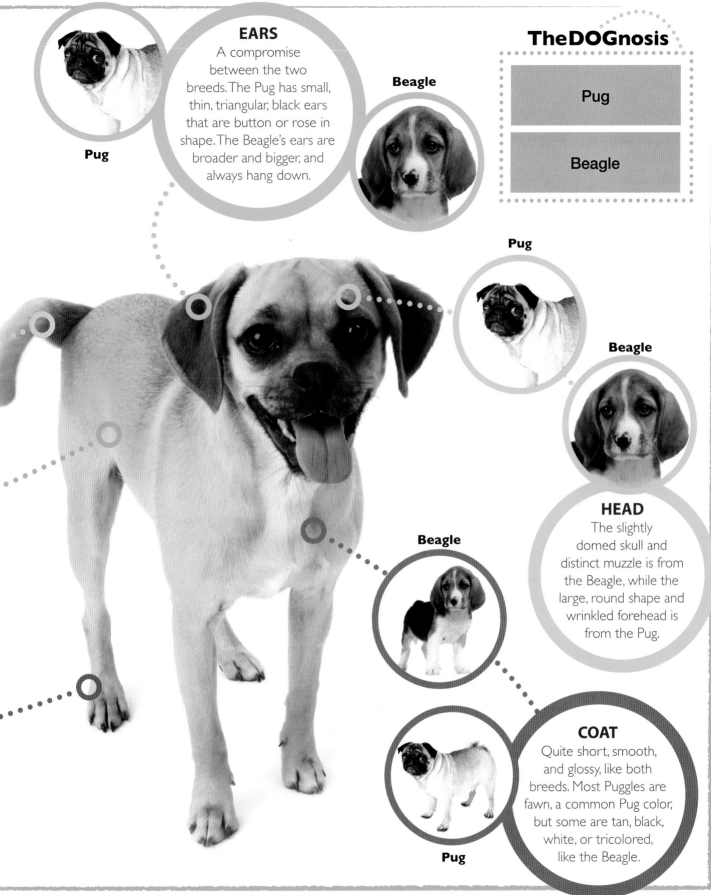

Pug

EARS
A compromise between the two breeds. The Pug has small, thin, triangular, black ears that are button or rose in shape. The Beagle's ears are broader and bigger, and always hang down.

Beagle

TheDOGnosis

Pug

Beagle

Pug

Beagle

HEAD
The slightly domed skull and distinct muzzle is from the Beagle, while the large, round shape and wrinkled forehead is from the Pug.

Beagle

COAT
Quite short, smooth, and glossy, like both breeds. Most Puggles are fawn, a common Pug color, but some are tan, black, white, or tricolored, like the Beagle.

Pug

Cockapoo

The Cockapoo is a Poodle-Cocker Spaniel cross. Poodles of all three sizes (Standard, Miniature, and Toy) may appear in her ancestry, as may both English and American Cocker Spaniels. The result is a dog who comes in several sizes but always has the cuddly look and super intelligence of the Poodle, and the patient disposition and sturdy build of the Cocker Spaniel. The resulting dog is very focused on her family, good with children, friendly with strangers, active but not hyper, and relatively easier to groom than either of her parent breeds. In Australia and northern Europe, these dogs are called Spoodles.

HEAD

Like a Cocker Spaniel's, the length of the muzzle just about matches the length of the skull, and the muzzle is not pointed. Like a Poodle's, the head is rounded on top and the face is broad with dark, wide-set eyes.

Miniature Poodle

Cocker Spaniel

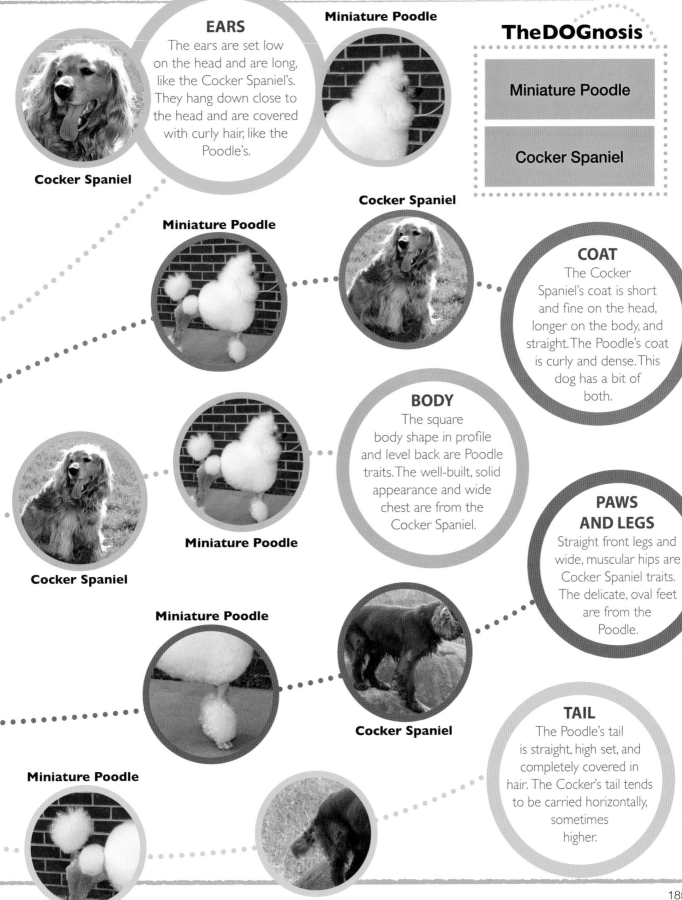

EARS
The ears are set low on the head and are long, like the Cocker Spaniel's. They hang down close to the head and are covered with curly hair, like the Poodle's.

Cocker Spaniel

Miniature Poodle

TheDOGnosis

Miniature Poodle

Cocker Spaniel

Cocker Spaniel

Miniature Poodle

COAT
The Cocker Spaniel's coat is short and fine on the head, longer on the body, and straight. The Poodle's coat is curly and dense. This dog has a bit of both.

BODY
The square body shape in profile and level back are Poodle traits. The well-built, solid appearance and wide chest are from the Cocker Spaniel.

Cocker Spaniel

Miniature Poodle

PAWS AND LEGS
Straight front legs and wide, muscular hips are Cocker Spaniel traits. The delicate, oval feet are from the Poodle.

Miniature Poodle

Cocker Spaniel

TAIL
The Poodle's tail is straight, high set, and completely covered in hair. The Cocker's tail tends to be carried horizontally, sometimes higher.

Miniature Poodle

Cocker Spaniel

Schnoodle

This Schnoodle is a cross between a Miniature Schnauzer and a Miniature Poodle. Because Poodles come in three sizes and Schnauzers come in two, you can find much bigger Schnoodles and slightly smaller ones. They all inherit the intelligence of both ancestral breeds, and tend to be very focused on the people in their family. They like to learn and they love to play games. They also like to run—but since they're small, you don't need to take them jogging all afternoon to tire them out. Their coat does not shed as much as other breeds, but grows continuously. This requires weekly brushing and a trim every two or three months to make sure matting does not become an issue.

HEAD
On the Schnauzer, the top part of the skull is long but the muzzle is not too long and ends bluntly. The wide face, very dark eyes set wide apart, and moderately rounded skull are from the Poodle.

Miniature Schnauzer

Miniature Poodle

TheDOGnosis

Miniature Poodle

Miniature Schnauzer

EARS
These are mostly Schnauzer ears: high set, small, V-shaped, and folding close to the skull. But the furriness comes from the Poodle.

Miniature Poodle

Miniature Schnauzer

Miniature Poodle

BODY
Short and deep, with a straight topline that declines slightly from the shoulders to the tail, like the Schnauzer's. Square body shape in profile, with a deep and moderately wide chest, like the Poodle's.

Miniature Schnauzer

COAT
The double coat, with a wiry outercoat and softer undercoat, is like the Schnauzer's. That gray closer to the body is a Schnauzer color underneath. But the hair is softer and longer than the Schnauzer's—that's the Poodle influence.

Miniature Schnauzer

Miniature Poodle

Miniature Schnauzer

Miniature Poodle

PAWS AND LEGS
The Poodle has small, oval feet, cushioned on thick pads. The Schnauzer has strong, straight legs set wide apart.

Index